The New Food Lover's Companion, Third Edition

The New Food Lover's Tiptionary, Second Edition

The Ultimate Liquor-Free Drink Guide

The Ultimate A-to-Z Bar Guide

The Wine Lover's Companion

Never Eat More Than You Can Lift

The Joy of Cookies

The Food Lover's Guide to Chocolate and Vanilla

The Food Lover's Guide to Meat and Potatoes

The New Breads, Second Edition

Cooking Smart

Simply Sensational Desserts

THE ULTIMATE GUIDE TO PITCHER DRINKS

THE
Ultimate Guide
TO Pitcher Drinks

COOL COCKTAILS FOR A CROWD

Sharon Tyler Herbst

Villard New York

Library of Congress Cataloging-in-Publication Data
Herbst, Sharon Tyler.
    The ultimate guide to pitcher drinks: cool cocktails for
    a crowd / Sharon Tyler Herbst.
        p.   cm.
    Includes index.
    ISBN 0-8129-6768-2
    1. Cocktails.   I. Title.
    TX951 .H544 2003
    641.8'74—dc21   2002033851

Book design and illustrations by Barbara M. Bachman

TO TAMMY CABOT, BECAUSE
SHE'S SO CREATIVE AND CLEVER,
ESPECIALLY WITH BOOK IDEAS

acknowledgments

Rarely have I had so much fun writing a book, in part because friends, family, and neighbors were practically standing in line to be tasters. And it's clear to me now that sharing a pitcher or two creates a bond unlike any other.

First of all, thanks, as always, to my adorable husband, Ron, my Rock-of-Gibraltar hero, my everything.

A huge hug goes to pal Tammy Cabot at Random House, who "pitchered" the concept for this book and believed I was the one to create it. My only regret is that she was on the other side of the continent and couldn't partake in all the tasting.

A big thanks to a small group of particularly spirited tasters: Lee and Susan Janvrin (dear friends who sampled more pitcherfuls than any of us want to admit), Linda Garcia and Greg Rockwell, Margot Oven and Doug Howell, and Ron and Sara Ryba.

Thanks also to Emery Van Hook, Lee Anne Garner, and Christine Miller, all of whom enthusiastically contributed drink ideas.

Too far away to taste, but always there for me in spirit: Kay and Wayne Tyler (dearest Mom and Dad), Tia and Jim McCurdy (sweet sister and brother-in-law), Tyler and Andrew Leslie, Leslie Bloom, Beth Casey, Daniel Maye, Phillip Cooke, Sue and Gene Bain, Dickie and Leslie Brennan,

Walt and Carol Boice, Emma Swain and Wes Jones, the Herbsts—Barry, Kathy, Brian, Gabe, Joyce, and Lew, and Julie and Ron Goodlin.

And at Villard: Senior editor Mary Bahr, with whom I was immediately simpatico—she's creative and wise and fought like a tiger for what we wanted; Mary's ever helpful editorial assistant, Laura Ford; detail maven and production editor Vincent La Scala, for massaging this book into shape; book designer Barbara Bachman, who created this book's "look"; production manager Richard Elman, who brings it all together; publicity wizard Jynne Martin, who gets the word out; and the dozens of behind-the-scenes people who labor tirelessly and without fanfare to make Villard's books the best they can be.

Cheers to one and all!

CONTENTS

part two

*I generally avoid temptation—
unless I can't resist it.*

—MAE WEST, AMERICAN ACTRESS

No doubt about it, cocktails stimulate good times, animate parties, and break the ice. But who wants to miss out on the fun by mixing drinks, one by one? Well, that's a no-brainer. We'd all rather be partying with our friends. Which is why making and serving drinks in a pitcher is an idea whose time has come—in fact, it's way overdue.

Pitcher drinks are stylish, fun, and easy, take the angst out of entertaining, and add sass and spontaneity to gatherings large and small. Bottom line: A premixed pitcher of spirited refreshment is a huge asset to any party.

The Ultimate Guide to Pitcher Drinks has over 155 lively pitcher-drink recipes ranging from high- to low-alcohol and even a few buzz-free libations. In these pages, you'll find recipes for classics like Martinis and Manhattans, newer favorites like Kamikazes and Mudslides, soothing sips like Summer Hummer and Muchas Smoochas, tropical tempters like Cosmic Coconut and Rum Rush, sparklers like Brandied Apple Fizz and French Flirt, international raves from Brazil's Caipirinha to Cuba's Mojito, sweet treats such as Banana Split and Green Genie, and colorful concoctions like Liquid Oxygen and Déjà Blue. There's something here for every mood and every party—the only equipment you need is a pitcher and a long-handled spoon and you're in business.

Besides great recipes, this book has loads of tips on techniques, ingredients, equipment, glassware, garnishes, measurements, responsible drinking, and hangover helpers (no, Virginia, there is no cure). Plus, there's a chapter on party-food ideas for people who don't like to cook.

The *Ultimate Guide to Pitcher Drinks* is the ideal book for today's easy entertaining. It has all the ingredients anyone needs to create a fantastic pitcher-perfect party. Add a new dimension to entertaining and become a twenty-first-century host with these fun and spirited pitcher drinks. They'll be the hit of the party and the party will positively be a hit with your friends.

Cheers!

Part One

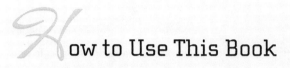

ow to Use This Book

There's also a chapter on party food for people who don't like to cook—**Effortless Eats** (pages 181–198).

CROSS-REFERENCES are indicated by SMALL CAPITALS, pointing to the definitions in **Bar Banter** (pages 7–33).

DIRECTORY OF DRINKS BY CATEGORY (pages 70–75) gives you at-a-glance access to recipes by style and potency. The headings are: Classic Cocktails and Drinks, Popular Favorites, Tropical Tempters, Sparkling Sippers, Dessert in a Glass, Potent Concoctions (High Alcohol), In the Mood (Moderate Alcohol), Easy Does It (Low to Moderate Alcohol), and Buzz-Free Zone (Liquor-Free).

DRINK RECIPES (pages 76–178) are arranged in a user-friendly A-to-Z format. Referring to either the Directory of Drinks by Category (pages 70–75) or the Index (pages 199–209) will lead you to just the drink you want. But if you know what you want—such as a Martini—you can find it easily alphabetically.

RECIPE INGREDIENTS are listed first for home use (tablespoons, cups), then in fluid ounces for bartenders looking for pitcher panache.

ICE CUBES are standard size, not miniature.

WATER IS ADDED in those recipes where single-drink preparations are classically shaken with ice, which melts slightly and contributes water to the drink.

THE INDEX (pages 199–209) is particularly extensive, listing recipes by the name of the drink, as well as by the drink's primary ingredients.

Th-th-that's all, folks. Now go party hearty with these fun party drinks!

A grasshopper hops into a bar and the

bartender says,

"Hey, there's a drink named after you."

The grasshopper exclaims in surprise,

"You gotta be kiddin'—there's a drink

named Ralph?"

*I*ngredients and Terms

ABSENTE [AB-sent] **Called "Absinthe refined" by the producer, Absente is the most recent proxy for the forbidden ABSINTHE. Instead of the toxic wormwood, Absente contains southernwood** (petite absinthe), which is said to contribute the more authentic flavor of the original. Absente's primary flavor hit is anise, but there are myriad herbs that contribute to its multifaceted palate. The clear, pale-green color of this LIQUEUR turns opaque when mixed with water. Absente is a powerful 55 percent alcohol, which is still considerably less than the 68 percent absinthe. Substitutes for Absente include PERNOD, ouzo, and anisette.

ABSINTHE [AB-sinth] A green, anise-flavored LIQUEUR that was banned in the United States and other countries in the early twentieth century because it contains wormwood, which is toxic when taken in quantity. If that weren't enough, this French potable is a potent 68 percent alcohol. It was the wormwood–high octane fusion that prompted many in the nineteenth-century Parisian artistic community (such as Degas, Toulouse-Lautrec, and Oscar Wilde) to nickname it the "green muse." Among the many absinthe substitutes are ABSENTE, anisette, ouzo, and PERNOD.

ALCOHOL Although used generally to specifically describe any alcoholic liquor, alcohol is a DISTILLATION of the fermented (*see* FERMENTATION) essence of grains, fruits, or vegetables. The result is a clear, intoxicating liquid. *See also* LIQUOR.

ALIZÉ [ah-lee-ZAY] A French LIQUEUR based on Cognac and passion fruit juice. There are three variations of Alizé, all of which are a relatively low 16 percent alcohol. The original blend, **Alizé Gold Passion**, is yellow in color and has a refreshing passion fruit flavor with hints of apricots, citrus, and peaches. **Alizé Red Passion** has the addition of cranberry and other juices, which contribute a red color and tangy flavor. **Alizé Wild Passion** has a tropical sunset hue and a flavor combination of passion fruit juices, mango, and pink grapefruit. The word *alizé* means "a gentle trade wind."

AMARETTO [am-ah-REHT-toh] An amber-colored, almond-flavored LIQUEUR, typically flavored with apricot-pit kernels. Originally from Italy, amaretto's now also produced in the United States and other countries. Depending on the producer, this liqueur can range in alcohol from about 21 to 28 percent.

APÉRITIF [ah-perhr-ih-TEEF] A drink (typically light in alcohol) consumed before a meal. Apéritifs can be a single potable, such as CHAMPAGNE or LILLET, or a mixed drink.

APPLE BRANDY A generic term for any BRANDY made from apple cider. Most apple brandies aren't sweet, like a LIQUEUR, but are distilled (*see* DISTILLATION) DRY at 40 percent alcohol. In the United States, such spirits are called *applejack.* Apple brandy has a very subtle apple flavor. The world's most renowned example is CALVADOS.

APRICOT BRANDY A DISTILLATE made from apricots or pure apricot juice with a typical alcohol range of between 20 and 24 percent. Apricot brandy has a fruity aroma and flavor but is DRY, unlike a sweet apricot-flavored LIQUEUR. Peach brandy may be substituted. *See also* BRANDY.

BANANA-FLAVORED LIQUEUR *see* CRÈME DE BANANA

BITTERS A bitter to bittersweet DISTILLATION of a complex blend of aromatic plants (herbs, barks, flowers, seeds, roots). Some bitters taste distinctively of their base ingredient (such as apricot, orange, or peach), and are named accordingly. Among the more popular bitters are Angostura (named for its angostura-bark base) and Peychaud's (named for its inventor). Because the flavor of bitters is so intense, a little goes a long way.

BLEND n. An alcoholic beverage created from two or more DISTILLATES. For example, blended whiskey is a combination of two or more 100-proof straight whiskeys blended with neutral spirits.

BOURBON An American corn-based WHISKEY made with a MASH-grain that's ground or crushed before being steeped in hot water and fermented (*see* FERMENTATION). Its name comes from the fact that it originated in Bourbon County, Kentucky. **Straight bourbon** is made from a mash that contains between 51 and 79 percent corn. **Corn whiskey** is made from a mash that contains over 80 percent corn. **Single-barrel bourbon** means just that—it comes from a single barrel. The term **small-batch bourbon** describes a high-quality BLEND of bourbons from selected barrels and of different maturity levels, and doesn't necessarily mean that a small amount was produced. The alcohol content of bourbon can range from 40 to 50 percent.

BRANDY In the most basic terms, brandy is a LIQUOR distilled (*see* DISTILLATION) from wine (grapes) or other fermented fruit juice. Some of the finest brandies (Cognac and Armagnac) hail from southwestern France. Other fruits popular for making brandy include apples (CALVADOS) and plums (slivovitz). Although some brandies are aged in oak (such as Armagnac, Calvados, and Cognac), most are not. The majority of brandies are 40 percent alcohol. *See also* APPLE BRANDY; APRICOT BRANDY.

BRUT *see* CHAMPAGNE

CACHAÇA [kah-SHAH-sah] The national spirit of Brazil, cachaça is a 40 percent alcohol DISTILLATE made from unrefined sugarcane. Its flavor is often described as a cross between TEQUILA and RUM, with a slightly smoky character. Cachaça is indispensable in Brazil's most popular drink, the Caipirinha (page 89). Although Brazil produces myriad brands of cachaça, those most readily available in the United States are **Pitù, Cachaça 51, Ypióca, Velho Barreiro,** and **Toucano Gold** (a cachaça "rum" that's been aged two years in oak casks).

CALVADOS [KAL-vah-dohs] Considered one of the world's greatest brandies, Calvados comes from the Normandy region in France. This BRANDY is made from apple cider, which gives it a perfumy apple scent. Its rich flavor and body come from aging in Limousin oak for two to five years or more. Calvados is 40 percent alcohol.

CANE SYRUP An extremely thick, sweet syrup made from the juice extracted from sugarcane. Cane syrup has a characteristic sugarcane aroma and flavor. It ranges in color from dark gold to dark brown and can be found in natural food stores, Caribbean and Creole markets, and some supermarkets.

CANTON DELICATE GINGER LIQUEUR A ginger-flavored LIQUEUR made in southern China by Charles Jacquin et Cie. It's comprised of six different kinds of ginger, herbs, ginseng, and brandy. This ginger liqueur is 16.5 percent alcohol, isn't overly sweet, and has a subtle ginger flavor that doesn't bite.

CAVA [KAH-vah] A sparkling wine produced in the Catalan region in northeastern Spain. The word *cava* is Catalan for "cellar." The best cavas are those made with Chardonnay or Pinot Noir grapes. Most have an alcohol level of 12 percent.

CHAMBORD [sham-BORD] A black-raspberry-flavored, garnet-colored LIQUEUR made in France by the American-French company Charles Jacquin et Cie. There's really no flavor substitute for the intensely flavored Chambord, which is a relatively low 16.5 percent alcohol.

CHAMPAGNE [sham-PAYN] Although most of us have fallen into the habit of calling any sparkling wine "champagne," *true* Champagne comes only from France's Champagne region, northeast of Paris. Most countries acknowledge French tradition by calling their sparklers by other names: *Sekt* in Germany, *spumante* in Italy, *cava* in Spain, and simply "sparkling wine" in the United States (although some producers are stepping on convention and labeling their sparklers "champagne"). Look for a sparkling wine with "*méthode champenoise*" on the label, which indicates that the wine has undergone a second FERMENTATION in the bottle, a traditional French method that produces superior sparkling wines. **Vintage champagnes** are produced from the best grapes and must be aged three years before being released. **Nonvintage champagnes** (the majority of those available) are blends of wine from two or more years.

Blanc de blancs sparklers are made entirely from Chardonnay grapes and have a pale-blond color. **Blanc de noirs** describes wines made with Pinot Noir grapes (sometimes Meunier), which confer a pale apricot to pink hue. The label will tell you the sparkler's sweetness level: **extra-brut** is bone-DRY, under 0.6 percent sugar (you won't find many of these on the shelves); **brut** is very dry (less than 1.5 percent sugar) and is what's most commonly available; **extra-sec** or **extra-dry** is slightly sweeter; **sec** is medium-sweet; **demi-sec** is sweet; and **doux** is very sweet. Most drink recipes call for brut or extra-dry. Champagnes typically have an alcohol content of 12 percent.

CHERRIES, MARASCHINO *see* page 45

CLUB SODA Water that's been injected with carbon dioxide, which makes it bubbly. Club soda gets its slightly salty-citric flavor from small amounts of added sodium bicarbonate and sodium citrate. For those who don't like that flavor (like me), SELTZER WATER makes a much cleaner-tasting mixer. Club soda is also called *soda water. See also* TONIC WATER; WATER.

COCONUT MILK An unsweetened, milky liquid made by processing water with coconut meat. It's sold in regular and low-fat versions. Although once only available in Asian markets, coconut milk can now be found in many supermarkets, generally in the "ethnic" section. Some Asian markets also carry a thicker, more concentrated **coconut cream,** which is unsweetened and not to be confused with the exceedingly sweet CREAM OF COCONUT.

COCONUT RUM *see* MALIBU COCONUT RUM

COINTREAU [KWAHN-troh] Considered by many to be the world's most distinguished orange LIQUEUR, Cointreau is colorless, crystal-clear, and has an exotic, mildly bitter orange flavor. It's flavored with the peel from two types of orange—sour oranges from the Caribbean island of Curaçao and sweet oranges from Spain. Cointreau's alcohol content is 40 percent. *See also* CURAÇAO; TRIPLE SEC.

CORDIAL *see* LIQUEUR

CREAM There are two types of cream used in the recipes in this book—heavy cream and half-and-half. **Heavy** (or **whipping**) **cream** is about 40 percent milk fat and gives drinks a smooth, silky texture and body. **Half-and-half** is a mixture of half milk and half cream. It has only about 12 percent milk fat and adds a lightly creamy texture and flavor.

CREAM OF COCONUT A thick, extremely sweet blend of coconut paste, water, and sugar. Cream of coconut is available in supermarkets and liquor stores. *See also* COCONUT MILK.

CRÈME DE BANANA; CRÈME DE BANANE [krehm deuh bah-NA-nuh (-NAHN)] A clear, bright yellow LIQUEUR (24 percent alcohol) with an intensely sweet, banana flavor.

CRÈME DE CACAO [krehm deuh kah-KAH-oh] A chocolate-flavored LIQUEUR with a clear, dark brown color. **White crème de cacao** is clear and colorless but tastes the same. Crème de cacao is 24 percent alcohol.

CUARENTA Y TRES [kwah-RAYN-tah ee TRAYSS] *see* LICOR 43

CURAÇAO [KYOOR-uh-soh] A generic term for orange-flavored LIQUEURS flavored with the dried peel of bitter oranges native to Curaçao, an island in the southern Caribbean. Most curaçaos are amber in color, some are tinted blue, and a few are colorless. Curaçaos can range in alcohol from 23 to 40 percent. *See also* COINTREAU; TRIPLE SEC.

DISTILLATE; DISTILLATION n. Any alcoholic beverage that has undergone DISTILLATION, such as BRANDY, GIN, RUM, TEQUILA, VODKA, and WHISKEY.

DISTILLATION The process of purifying and/or concentrating a liquid through several steps of evaporation and subsequent collection of the condensation.

DRY A term used in the world of WINE and SPIRITS to describe a potable that isn't sweet. For sparkling wine sweetness designations, *see* CHAMPAGNE. *See also* SEC.

FERMENTATION A process in which the enzymes from yeast convert natural sugars in grain, fruit, and vegetables into ALCOHOL. For example, yeast converts the sugars in grape juice for WINE, those in sugarcane molasses for RUM, and the starch in grains (subsequently converted into sugar by diastase enzymes) for WHISKEY.

FLOAT n. A small amount of liquid (such as 151-PROOF rum) that floats atop another liquid without being mixed in. **float v.** To slowly and steadily pour a liquid over the back of a spoon onto the surface of another liquid. The spoon is used to break the "fall" of the topping liquid, distributing it evenly onto the liquid below so that it floats rather than immediately blending in.

FLOWERS *see* page 48

FRUIT JUICES; FRUIT NECTARS There are loads of fruit juices on supermarket shelves and in the freezer section, and most of them are fine. The one exception is bottled lemon and lime juice, which in no way compares to the flavor of fresh. So, come on, guys, don't be lazy. Get out that JUICER (page 39) and go to it. Your drinks will thank you for it—so will your guests. Fresh orange juice is also preferable, providing it's flavorful. Bottom line: Sometimes orange juice made from frozen concentrate simply has more taste. *See also* Squeeze Play, page 113; Lemon Logic, page 142.

GALLIANO; LIQUORE GALLIANO [gal-LYAH-noh] A brilliant yellow Italian LIQUEUR (40 percent alcohol) flavored with spices, herbs, and flowers. This sweet, syrupy elixir has a spicy-herbal flavor reminiscent of licorice.

GARNISHES see pages 43–53

GIN A clear, colorless LIQUOR made from grain. Gin undergoes two DISTILLATIONS—first to achieve the desired level of alcohol, then again to flavor the liquor with botanicals. Juniper berries are the primary flavoring for gin, but others include angelica, anise, cardamom, cassia bark, fennel, and ginger. There are two styles of gin. The more popular of the two is **dry gin**, made primarily from corn, with a small percentage of malted barley and other grains. Aromatic dry gins have a moderately light body and flavor. English-made dry gins are typically more flavorful and slightly higher in alcohol than those made in the United States. Label terms such as "English Dry Gin" and "London Dry Gin" describe the gin's style, not where it was produced. There are also dry gins flavored with everything from grapefruit to mint, and labeled accordingly. The second style of gin is **Dutch gin,** also known as *Hollands, Genever,* and *Jenever.* The full-flavored, slightly sweet and malty Dutch gins are customarily comprised of equal parts of malted barley, corn, and rye. Most gins are 40 percent alcohol.

GOLDSCHLÄGER [GOLT-shlah-gehr] **A Swiss** schnapps LIQUEUR with an intense tangy-sweet cinnamon flavor and a hot bite on the finish. The thick, syrupy Goldschläger (43.5 percent alcohol) is colorless and clear with floating bits of edible gold leaf, which aren't particularly discernible on the palate.

GRAND MARNIER [GRAN mahr-NYAY] **An amber-colored, orange-flavored** LIQUEUR made in France. Grand Marnier is Cognac-based, flavored with vanilla, spices, and bitter orange peel, and 38.5 percent alcohol.

GRENADINE SYRUP; GRENADINE [GREHN-uh-deen] **A sweet, red, nonalcoholic syrup with an exotic pomegranate flavor. Although once made solely from Caribbean pomegranates, grenadine is now typically made with other fruit juice concentrates. Grenadine is used to sweeten and flavor drinks.**

HALF-AND-HALF *see* CREAM

ICE A drink's flavor can be ruined with bad-tasting ice, and ice can only taste as good as the water from which it's made. Sample your water—if it's highly chlorinated or otherwise off-tasting, use packaged ice, which is available crushed or in cubes. Even if your water tastes fine, remember that ice easily absorbs odors from foods in the freezer, so taste any ice that's been in there a long time. *See also* WATER.

Ice cubes made with water that's been boiled and cooled will be clearer than those made with regular tap water. *See also* Decorative Ice Cubes, page 49; Flavored Ice Cubes, page 50.

Crushed ice should be used in drinks that call for it—ice cubes just won't contribute the right texture for drinks like Mint Julep (page 131). On the other hand, crushed ice melts much faster than ice cubes, diluting a drink more quickly, so don't use it if a recipe calls for ice cubes. You can either buy crushed ice, or make your own with one of the many inexpensive ice crushers on the market today (*see* ICE CRUSHER, page 38). Or release your aggressions by crushing it manually—seal ice cubes in a heavy-duty plastic bag, wrap the bag in a heavy towel, then whack away with a mallet, rolling pin, etc. Prepare crushed ice in advance and store in a plastic bag in the freezer.

IRISH CREAM LIQUEURS There are numerous Irish cream liqueurs on the market today. Bailey's was the original, but other popular brands include Brogan's, Carolans,

McCormick's, and St. Brendan's. They're all rich and sweet, and can range in color from oatmeal to caramel and in texture from creamy to milky. Depending on the brand, the flavor can be spicy, chocolaty, toffeelike, or honeyed. Most Irish cream liqueurs have an alcohol content in the 17 percent range.

KAHLÚA [kah-LOO-ah] The most popular coffee-flavored LIQUEUR in the world, Kahlúa has been produced in Mexico for over fifty years. It has a dark brown color and a complex coffee flavor with hints of dark chocolate and vanilla. This smooth elixir contains 26.5 percent alcohol.

LEMON JUICE; LIME JUICE *see* Squeeze Play, page 113; Lemon Logic, page 142.

LICOR 43 [lih-KOR] A bright yellow, extremely sweet and viscous LIQUEUR with an exotic citrusy flavor perfumed with vanilla and spices. It's also called *Cuarenta Y Tres* (Spanish for "forty-three"), owing to the fact that it's comprised of forty-three different ingredients blended from an ancient formula. This liqueur is 31 percent alcohol.

LILLET [lee-LAY; lih-LAY] A wine-based APÉRITIF blended with BRANDY, fruit, spices, and herbs. **Lillet Blanc** has a golden color and a flavor that reflects orange, honey, lime, and mint. **Lillet Rouge** is ruby red, slightly sweeter than the white version, and tastes of cherries, berries, vanilla, and spices. Lillet has an alcohol content of 18 percent.

LIMONCELLO [lee-mown-CHEL-LOH] Hailing from Sicily, this Italian LIQUEUR is a simple infusion of lemons and alcohol sweetened with sugar. It has a clean, pure lemon flavor and is perfect for après-dinner sipping. Keep it in the freezer and pour directly into small liqueur glasses. The alcohol content of most limoncellos is right around 30 percent.

LIQUEUR [lih-KYOOR; lih-KER] Also called *cordial,* a liqueur is a SPIRIT that's been flavored and sweetened. The spirit base can be almost anything (BRANDY, RUM, VODKA, WHISKEY, and so on); the flavorings can be natural (fruits, flowers, herbs, seeds, spices, etc.) or artificial. You get what you pay for—quality brands use the finest ingredients, essential oils, and extracts; inexpensive products typically use artificial flavorings. **Cream liqueurs** get their smooth, velvety texture from stabilized cream. The alcohol content of liqueurs ranges from about 15 percent (for some IRISH CREAM LIQUEURS) to 55 percent (for green Chartreuse); a few liqueur blends (Kahlúa Mudslide, page 138) have only 6.5 percent alcohol.

LIQUOR A distilled (*see* DISTILLATION) alcoholic beverage, such as GIN, TEQUILA, VODKA, and WHISKEY. *See also* ALCOHOL; SPIRITS.

MALIBU; MALIBU COCONUT RUM A clear, moderately light-bodied, coconut-flavored rum. Malibu has a silky texture and spicy accents of almonds and mocha. Its alcohol content is 24 percent. There are other coconut-flavored rums, but Malibu is considered one of the best.

MARASCHINO CHERRIES *see* page 45

MASH Grain that's coarsely milled, mixed with hot water, and allowed to ferment (*see* FERMENTATION) in a large vat. Mash is used for both beer and whiskey. **Sweet mash** begins fermentation with fresh yeast; **sour mash** (for liquors such as BOURBON and Tennessee WHISKEY) combines fresh yeast with part of the previous fermentation.

MEZCAL; MESCAL [mehs-KAL] Originating in Oaxaca, Mexico, mezcal is a clear, potent liquor that, like TEQUILA, is produced from the agave plant. However, whereas tequila can only be made from blue agave grown in a specified area, mezcal can be made anywhere in Mexico and from any of eight agave species. For mezcal, the agave is baked in fire pits or underground ovens. This processing gives mezcal its characteristic smoky, peppery flavor. Spirits labeled *Mezcal de Gusanitos* contain a small worm (*gusano*), which lives on the agave plant and may be red or white, depending on the type of plant from which it comes. Legend tells us the worm honors and strengthens the person who swallows it. Most mezcals are 40 percent alcohol.

MIDORI [mih-DOOR-ee] A vibrant green LIQUEUR with a delicate melon flavor and 21 percent alcohol. It was created in Japan in the late seventies.

MUDDLE; MUDDLING The term "muddle" refers to mashing or crushing ingredients together (such as mint and sugar for a Mint Julep, page 131) to release flavors and essential oils. Muddling is typically done with a MUDDLER (page 39) but can also be done with the back of a wooden spoon.

NON-ALCOHOLIC TRIPLE SEC *see* ROSE'S NON-ALCOHOLIC TRIPLE SEC

ON THE ROCKS A bartender's term for a drink served over ice cubes. *See also* UP.

ORANGE FLOWER WATER A perfumy orange-flavored DISTILLATION of bitter-orange blossoms and water. It's available in supermarkets and liquor stores.

ORGEAT SYRUP [or-ZHAY] A sweet, nonalcoholic syrup with a light almond flavor. It's also known as *sirop d'amandes,* and is available in liquor stores and some supermarkets.

PARFAIT AMOUR; PARFAIT D'AMOUR [par-FAY ah-MOHR] French for "perfect love," parfait amour is a LIQUEUR (25 percent alcohol) that ranges in color from violet to electric purple. Its delicate, orange-based flavor has hints of rose petals (sometimes violets), almonds, and vanilla.

PEACH SCHNAPPS A sweet, peach-flavored, colorless SPIRIT with about 21 percent alcohol.

PERNOD [pehr-NOH] A clear French LIQUEUR with an assertive licorice flavor and 40 percent alcohol. When mixed with water, Pernod turns from clear to cloudy and from pale yellow-green to whitish.

PIMM'S NO. 1 Created in 1840 by Londoner James Pimm, this SPIRIT is a blend of gin, fruit extracts, and fine LIQUEURS flavored with herbs and spices. It has a pleasantly bittersweet flavor and is only 25 percent alcohol. Pimm's No. 1 is typically blended with ginger ale or lemon-lime soda for a refreshing APÉRITIF.

PROOF A SPIRIT's alcoholic content is also referred to as "proof," which equates to twice the amount of ALCOHOL. For example, a label that states "80 proof" tells you the contents are 40 percent alcohol. Some labels simply indicate the percentage of alcohol.

ROSE'S LIME JUICE **A bottled, sweetened, lime-flavored syrup made from juice concentrate. This clear, yellow-green mixer can be found in liquor stores and some supermarkets.**

ROSE'S NON-ALCOHOLIC TRIPLE SEC **A sweet, orange-flavored, alcohol-free version of TRIPLE SEC, available in liquor stores and some supermarkets.**

RUM **Born in the West Indies and now produced throughout the Caribbean and around the world, rum is a DISTILLATE produced from sugarcane. Once the juice is extracted from the sugarcane, it's boiled until reduced to a thick syrup, which is clarified. The syrup is then separated into crystallized sugar and molasses. The molasses is fermented (*see* FERMENTATION) with water and yeast before it undergoes DISTILLATION. Most rums are distilled to 40 percent alcohol. Light rums (also called *white* or *silver*) are light-bodied, DRY, and colorless, with a faint sweetness. Gold or amber rums are medium-bodied, richer-flavored, and have a golden color. Dark rums have a dark brown color, are full-bodied (in part because they're aged longer), and have a deep, rich caramel flavor, aroma, and texture. Jamaican rum is a marketing term for dark rums from that island. Demerara rum, a definitively rich and smoky dark rum produced in Guyana, is dark-colored, medium-bodied, and headily aromatic. It's bottled at both 40 percent and about 75** percent alcohol (151 PROOF). **Flavored rums** are typically light rums infused with ingredients like fruit, coconut, or spices. Among the more popular flavored rums today are Captain Morgan Original Spiced Rum and MALIBU.

RYE; RYE WHISKEY   A WHISKEY distilled (*see* DISTILLATION) from a MASH that, in the United States, must comprise a minimum of 51 percent rye (wheat and barley comprise much of the remaining formula). Rye whiskey must be aged in oak barrels for at least two years. It has a flavor similar to that of a rich BOURBON with an assertively spicy edge. Most ryes are 40 percent alcohol.

SCOTCH; SCOTCH WHISKY   A whisky (yes, without the "e") that is distilled and aged for three years (most are aged for five to ten years) in Scotland, although it may be bottled in other countries. **Malt Scotch whisky** is made from barley that's been malted (germinated or sprouted), which converts its starch to sugar. The smoky flavor so admired in malt whiskies comes from the malted barley being dried over peat fires. **Grain Scotch whisky,** used typically for blending, is made with a blend of malted barley and various unmalted grains—primarily corn, but also barley and wheat. **Blended Scotch** combines up to fifty different malt whiskies (plus grain whisky) to attain consistency of aroma and flavor. **Single-malt Scotch** is unblended malt whisky produced and bottled by a single distillery. The single-malt Scotch descriptors **Highlands Scotch** and **Lowlands Scotch** simply refer to geographical locations (draw a line across Scotland from Greenock to Dundee—the Highlands are above the line, the Lowlands below it).

SEC [SEHK] French for "dry." When used to depict still (nonsparkling) wines, *sec* has a literal translation—the wine is DRY, meaning it has little if any residual sugar. When describing sparkling wines, however, the word *sec* describes a wine that's relatively sweet; demi-sec is even sweeter. For sparkling wine sweetness designations, *see* CHAMPAGNE.

SELTZER WATER A flavorless, bubbly water that's more effervescent than many other sparkling waters. Seltzer water has a "clean" flavor because it's simply water charged with carbon dioxide. That's why I prefer it to CLUB SODA, which has a slightly salty flavor because it's been processed with sodium bicarbonate and sodium citrate. Seltzer water can be found in supermarkets and liquor stores. *See also* TONIC WATER; WATER.

SODA WATER see CLUB SODA

SOUTHERN COMFORT Created in 1874, Southern Comfort is the oldest American LIQUEUR made today. This 35 percent–alcohol, amber-colored SPIRIT is based on a highly guarded secret formula. Its flavor is smooth, spicy, and reminiscent of oranges and peaches.

SPIRIT(S) A general term for alcoholic beverages. *See also* ALCOHOL; LIQUOR.

SUGAR Superfine sugar (also called *ultrafine sugar* and *baker's sugar*) is used in this book because it dissolves quickly in cold liquids. It's commonly available in supermarkets.

SUPERFINE SUGAR *see* SUGAR

SWEETENED LIME JUICE *see* ROSE'S LIME JUICE

TEQUILA [teh–KEE–luh] A SPIRIT made from the DISTILLATION of the juice of blue agave plants (no other agave is permissible for tequila) grown in a precisely delineated area in the five Mexican states of Guanajuato, Jalisco, Michoacán, Nayarit, and Tamaulipas. Tequila must comprise at least 51 percent blue agave; the remaining 49 percent is typically sugarcane. Tequilas labeled "100% Blue Agave" are generally the best. There are four categories of tequila. **Silver tequila** (also known as *blanco, white,* or *plata*), which is bottled soon after distillation, has a smooth, fresh flavor with an herbaceous, peppery quality. **Gold tequila** (also called *joven abocado*) is a silver tequila with flavoring and coloring added (typically from caramel); it doesn't have to be aged. **Reposado tequila** may also have added flavoring and coloring; it's aged in wood for a minimum of two months and for up to a year. The aging produces a mellower character and adds hints of vanilla and spice to the flavor. **Añejo tequila** has been aged for at least one (often two to three) years, which produces a spirit with a smooth, elegant, complex flavor. *See also* MEZCAL.

TONIC WATER Effervescent carbon-dioxide-charged water flavored with fruit extracts, sugar, and a soupçon of the bitter alkaloid quinine. Tonic water (sometimes called *quinine* water) comes in regular and diet forms. *See also* CLUB SODA; SELTZER WATER.

TRIPLE SEC An elegant, orange-flavored LIQUEUR made with the peels of both sweet and bitter oranges. Although the name means "triple DRY," this smooth spirit is fruity and sweet. Triple sec is 30 percent alcohol. *See also* COINTREAU; CURAÇAO; ROSE'S NON-ALCOHOLIC TRIPLE SEC.

TUACA [too-AH-kah] A 35 percent–alcohol, honey-colored LIQUEUR made from a secret formula over five hundred years old. The brandy-based Tuaca has a vanilla-orange flavor reminiscent of butterscotch.

U P   Bartender's term for a drink served without ice, such as a Cosmopolitan (page 94). *See also* ON THE ROCKS.

VERMOUTH [ver-MOOTH]   A wine-based SPIRIT that's been fortified (with BRANDY or other neutral spirit) and flavored with myriad botanicals, including herbs, spices, and flowers. Each vermouth producer has its own exclusive recipe. Although all vermouth is made from white wine, there are two distinctive styles—sweet and DRY. **Dry vermouth** (also called *French vermouth*) has a pale golden color and an herbal flavor. It's popular for APÉRITIFS and as an ingredient in dry cocktails, such as the Martini (page 124). **Sweet vermouth** (also called *Italian-style vermouth*) has caramel added, which gives it a reddish-brown color and slightly sweet flavor. It's also used for apéritifs as well as for slightly sweet cocktails like the Manhattan (page 118). Once opened, vermouth should be stored in the refrigerator, as it will begin to lose flavor. It can be refrigerated for at least three months (some companies claim six months). Vermouths can range in alcohol from 15 to 20 percent.

VODKA   A clear, colorless LIQUOR that can be a DISTILLATION of grain, vegetables, or even fruit. Grain vodkas (made primarily from barley and wheat, sometimes rye or corn) are considered by many to be superior to those made from vegetables, such as potatoes and beets. Vodka's clarity is the result of the

distilled spirit being filtered through activated charcoal to remove any trace of impurity. Those who think vodka is flavorless
should taste this spirit at room temperature, which is the best
way to pick up subtle flavor nuances and distinctive character-
istics. **Flavored vodkas** can be infused with various ingredients,
such as coffee beans, herbs, fruit, and even chili peppers. Most
such vodkas are DRY, a few are sweetened. Vodka is commonly
40 percent alcohol, though some flavored versions can be as
low as 30 percent. The word "vodka" comes from the Russian
zhizennia voda, meaning "water of life," though there's dispute
on whether vodka originated in Russia or Poland.

WATER   A simple thing like water can make a huge difference in the taste of a drink. Bottom line: If your water doesn't
taste good, neither will anything made with it, from drinks to
ice cubes. If that's the case, use bottled distilled or spring
water for drinks or ice. *See also* CLUB SODA; ICE; SELTZER
WATER; TONIC WATER.

WHISKEY;   WHISKY   [HWIHSK-ee;   WIHSK-ee]
The name of this alcoholic DISTILLATE comes from the Celtic
(Gaelic) *uisqebaugh* (pronounced oos-kee-BAW or whis-kee-
BAW), which means "water of life." Traditionally, whiskies made
in Scotland and Canada are spelled "whisky," without the "e."
Whiskey is made from fermented MASH (typically of barley,
corn, oats, rye, or wheat). **Straight whiskey** (such as BOURBON

and RYE) is made from at least 51 percent of a grain and must be aged in oak barrels for two years. If straight whiskeys from different distilleries or distilling periods are blended, they must be labeled as such ("blended bourbon whiskey"). **Blended whiskey** is a combination of two or more straight whiskeys blended with neutral spirits or grain spirits. *See also* SCOTCH.

W I N E The naturally fermented (*see* FERMENTATION) juice of fruit—most commonly grapes, although wine is made from other fruits and even vegetables and grains. There are several categories of wine. **Sparkling wine** (such as CHAMPAGNE) contains bubbles of carbon dioxide gas, which can be produced naturally in the bottle, or through injection. **Still wine**, whether red, white, or rosé, is simply a descriptor for any nonsparkling wine. **Fortified wine** (such as sherry or port) has been augmented with BRANDY or other spirits. **Aromatic wine** (such as VERMOUTH) has been flavored with botanicals. **Dealcoholized wine** (also called *alcohol-free wine* and *nonalcoholic wine*) has been processed to remove the alcohol. It contains less than 0.5 percent alcohol and has less than half the calories of regular wine.

Some men are like musical glasses—

to produce their finest tones you

must keep them wet.

—SAMUEL TAYLOR COLERIDGE,
BRITISH POET, CRITIC

Equipment—Gadgets, Gizmos, and Glassware

HAVING THE RIGHT "STUFF" ON HAND WHEN you're making pitcher drinks just makes life easier. Following are a few gadgets that'll help the cause.

CHAMPAGNE STOPPER A neat gadget that can retain a sparkling wine's effervescence for at least twenty-four hours. This special stopper has a spring-loaded plug with two metal wings that fold down and over the neck of a champagne bottle, securing it against the force of the carbon dioxide gas and making it airtight.

CITRUS REAMER *see* JUICER

CITRUS SPOUT; LEMON SPOUT A great little tool for times you only need a small amount of juice. It's shaped like a tube about three inches long with a three-quarter-inch diameter. The end that screws into the lemon (orange, grapefruit) is saw-toothed; the other end is a covered spout (some have a built-in strainer). You simply screw the jagged end into the fruit, twisting until it's inserted, then squeeze out the juice. Wrap the fruit (spout in place) in a plastic bag and refrigerate until you need a little more juice. For information on how to get maximum juice from citrus, *see* Squeeze Play (page 113). *See also* JUICER.

CITRUS STRIPPER; STRIPPER A stainless-steel tool with a notched edge that cuts one-quarter-inch-wide strips from citrus rinds (it'll also cut channels in cucumbers, radishes, you name it). It's a great tool for making quick work of lemon twists (page 53). *See also* CITRUS ZESTER; VEGETABLE PEELER.

CITRUS ZESTER; ZESTER A tool specially designed to remove citrus zest (outer colored portion). It has a stainless-steel cutting edge with five tiny holes that, as the tool is drawn across the fruit, create threadlike strips of peel. Some zesters also have a "citrus stripper" notch on the side of the zester. I don't think it works as well as using a separate CITRUS STRIPPER with the notching edge on the tip. *See also* VEGETABLE PEELER.

COCKTAIL NAPKINS Have plenty on hand—at least three per person, just in case.

COCKTAIL PICKS These essentials are typically either wooden or plastic and come in all shapes and sizes. The most commonly available are colored plastic picks with some kind of decoratively shaped tip. The most colorful picks have frilly cellophane "hats" of various colors. Cocktail picks can be used for everything from drink garnishes to hors d'oeuvres.

CUTTING BOARD You'll want one on hand for cutting lemon wedges and other garnishes. There are wooden and plastic cutting boards; the latter can go into a dishwasher. Choose a small board if you're short on space. Keep a cutting board from sliding around on a countertop by putting a damp dish towel (or several layers of dampened heavy-duty paper towel) underneath it.

FUNNEL You'll find a variety of funnels (from narrow- to wide-mouthed) everywhere from variety stores to supermarkets. Choose one that's dishwasher-safe. Funnels are handy for transferring liquids back into a bottle, from a pitcher to a jar, etc.

GLASSWARE Hey, it'd be great to have a bar full of glasses in every shape and size but, for most of us, that's just not realistic. Bottom line: If you have three basic shapes (tall, squat, and stemmed), you'll do fine. **Tall glasses,** if you only have one set, should hold at least 10 to 12 ounces and be straight-sided. If you already have similar but larger-capacity glasses, use them and simply add more ice cubes so the fill won't look skimpy. **Old-fashioned glasses** are short, squat, and hold anywhere from 6 to 8 ounces; a **double old-fashioned** can hold 12 ounces or more. **Cocktail glasses** or **Martini glasses** are long-stemmed and have a flared bowl. They can hold anywhere from 4 to 10 ounces—choose a medium size if you're buying new glasses. **Champagne flutes** are a nice extra if you have storage space. Choose one that holds about 8 ounces if you're buying new. **Wineglasses** are another good all-around vessel—choose a medium (10- to 12-ounce) size. If you have unlimited budget and storage, you might want some of the specialty glasses like those for Hurricanes and Margaritas.

ICE BUCKET AND TONGS (OR SCOOP) Though you can keep ice in a large bowl, an ice bucket will keep it colder longer. Tongs are a nice touch when adding ice cubes to drinks. An ice scoop works for both crushed and cubed ice.

ICE CRUSHER If you're lucky enough to have a freezer that dispenses crushed ice, skip this paragraph. If you're not, you should know that there are myriad relatively inexpensive ice crushers, from manual crank-styles to electric. You'll find them everywhere from variety to department stores. Or banish frustrations by making your own crushed ice. *See* Crushed Ice, page 20.

JUICER; CITRUS REAMER A must-have for squeezing fresh juice. There are dozens of styles, ranging from small, handheld reamers, to those that straddle a measuring cup and have a built-in strainer, to electric juicers. *See also* CITRUS SPOUT.

MEASURING CUPS There are two styles of measuring cups. **Dry measuring cups** typically come in a nested set holding from ⅛ cup to 1 cup. They can be plastic or metal, and are used for ingredients like sugar. **Liquid measuring cups** are single containers (usually glass, sometimes plastic) that range in size from 1 to 8 cups.

MEASURING SPOONS Don't count on silverware teaspoons and tablespoons to measure accurately. Buy measuring spoons, which typically come in a nested set of six, ranging from ⅛ teaspoon to 1 tablespoon.

MUDDLER A rodlike instrument with a broad, rounded or flattened end, which is used to crush ingredients like mint leaves, as for a Mint Julep (page 131). Muddlers are typically made of wood because it won't scratch glass. They're available in gourmet shops, bar-supply stores, and some kitchenware shops. *See also* MUDDLE, page 24.

PICKS *see* COCKTAIL PICKS

PITCHERS No doubt about it, pitchers are the most important piece of equipment for a pitcher-drink book. And there are hundreds of different styles and sizes out there. Pitchers can be made of glass, acrylic, pottery, and even metal. But if you're buying new, choose clear glass or acrylic so the drink's color and texture can be seen. Glass is heavier, of course, but acrylic scratches easily, so it's a trade-off. Pitchers come in all shapes and sizes (from 50- to 116-ounce and more), but if you're only buying one, go as large as you can find. The good news is that many pitchers are relatively inexpensive, meaning you might want to purchase several. Some pitchers have removable ice inserts that'll keep liquids cold without watering them down. Some even have lids, although plastic wrap works fine for covering pitcher drinks. If you don't care about looks, there are 1- to 2-gallon plastic jugs with spigots available in container stores and some variety stores. Bottom line: Choose a pitcher (or other container) in the size and shape that suits your style.

STRIPPER *see* CITRUS STRIPPER

VEGETABLE PEELER A simple tool found everywhere from supermarkets to hardware stores—good for making wide citrus-peel garnishes. *See also* CITRUS STRIPPER; CITRUS ZESTER.

ZESTER *see* CITRUS ZESTER

Garnishes and Other Fandangos

A GARNISH NOT ONLY JAZZES UP A DRINK'S LOOKS
with a pop of color, but it can also forecast what's
coming. A chunk of honeydew perched on a glass
rim predicts a melon-flavored sipper, a wedge of
lime says, "Here comes something sassy and tart."
Savory garnishes like scallion brushes and jicama
cutouts dress up drinks like Bloody Marys (page
81). Whatever garnish you add, remember: It's a
decoration, not dinner. Tarting up a drink with too
much garnish is tacky.

Food isn't the only way you can add pizzazz
to drinks. Try using frosty glasses (*see* The Big

Chill, page 128), Decorative Ice Cubes (page 49), and straws. Tiny paper umbrellas (available at specialty shops and liquor stores) or edible flowers instantly convey "tiki (tropical) drink." Following are some ideas for easy, fun ways to make your drinks look great.

BERRIES Make a slot for large berries (like strawberries and blackberries) to straddle a glass rim by cutting a slit from the tip to within ¼ inch of the stem end. Smaller berries (raspberries and blueberries) may be speared on a decorative pick and either propped across the glass rim or plopped into the drink.

BRUSHES; CELERY BRUSHES Depending on how long you want the brush, cut celery ribs in 2- to 5-inch pieces. Slit each one lengthwise at ¼-inch intervals to within 1 inch of the other end. **Scallion brushes:** Trim off a scallion's root end and most of the green portion. Use a sharp, pointed knife to thinly slash both ends at ⅛-inch intervals, leaving a 1-inch uncut space in the center. **Finishing brushes:** Refrigerate celery or scallion pieces in a bowl of ice water for 1 hour, or until the slashed tips curl. Blot dry with paper towel; refrigerate in a plastic bag until ready to use.

CARROT CURLS Use a VEGETABLE PEELER (page 41) to cut thin, wide strips the length of a large, washed carrot. Drop strips into a bowl of ice water for at least 1 hour, or until they curl. Blot dry with paper towel; refrigerate in a plastic bag until ready to use.

CHERRIES, MARASCHINO These ultrasweet cherries are packed in sugar syrup and come in both red and green. *Please* don't use the green ones, which should be reserved for fruitcakes meant to age at least half a century. Red maraschinos are traditional in some drinks—the Manhattan, for one—and add a tropical touch to others. Look for cherries with stems, which provide a good handle with which to retrieve the fruit from a drink. You can find maraschino cherries in supermarkets and liquor stores everywhere.

CHERRY TWISTS Use a VEGETABLE PEELER (page 41) to cut thin strips of lime or lemon peel, about $\frac{1}{2}$ inch wide and $1\frac{1}{2}$ inches long. Wrap around a stemless maraschino cherry, securing it with a pick. *See also* CITRUS TWISTS; TWISTS, GENERAL.

CHILE PEPPER FLOWERS Choose small, brightly colored chiles (red, green, or yellow) and wear latex gloves to protect your hands from the chile's volatile oils. With a sharp, pointed knife, cut each pepper from the tip to the stem end at about $\frac{3}{8}$-inch intervals. Remove the seeds and, if desired, trim the "petal" tips to form points. Place in a bowl of ice water for 1 hour, or until the chiles open into flower shapes. Blot with paper towel; refrigerate in a plastic bag until ready to use.

CITRUS TWISTS The easiest way to produce lemon or other twists is by using a CITRUS STRIPPER (page 36), carving the rind from tip to tip. Although the strips won't be as narrow, you can also use a sharp paring knife or vegetable peeler to pare off thin, $1/2$-inch-wide strips. Before dropping a twist into a drink, hold it at both ends, colored part down, and give it a twist just above the drink to release a spray of citrus oil into the liquid's surface. You can also add flavor by rubbing the rim of the glass with the peel before twisting. *See also* CHERRY TWISTS; TWISTS, GENERAL.

COCOA POWDER; COCOA MIX Mocha- or chocolate-flavored drinks can be enhanced with a light sprinkling of chocolate powder. **Cocoa powder** is unsweetened and bitter, with a pure chocolate flavor. **Cocoa mix** (also called *instant cocoa*) is a combination of cocoa powder, dry milk, and sugar, and has a sweet milk-chocolate flavor. To get a nice light dusting of cocoa powder or mix on a drink, put it in a clean salt-shaker. Or put the powder in a fine sieve and lightly shake it over the drink.

CUTOUTS Use a cookie or canapé cutter to cut designs out of ⅛- to ¼-inch-thick slices of fruits (apples, peaches) or vegetables (carrots, cucumbers, jicama). Or simply use a sharp, pointed knife to make free-form cutouts.

DECORATED GLASS RIMS Coating glass rims with salt or sugar is a classic garnish for drinks like Margaritas (page 120) and Cosmopolitans (page 94). Start by dipping the glass rim in liquor, liqueur, or fruit juice, shaking off any excess liquid. The glass rim can also be dampened by simply dipping your fingertip into a liquid, then running it around the glass rim, or by rubbing the glass rim with a lemon, lime, or orange wedge. Have a plate of salt or granulated sugar standing by; dip the moist glass rim into it. Using kosher salt or coarse-grained decorating sugar will make a showier garnish; for festive occasions, use multicolored sugar. Set the salt- or sugar-decorated glasses upright; store in the freezer or refrigerator if you have room.

Zested glass rims: For a particularly jazzy decoration, embellish glass rims with **sugared** or **salted citrus zest.** On a plate, combine equal parts sugar or salt and finely grated lemon, lime, or orange zest (the outer colored portion of the rind). The amount needed depends on the number of and width of the glass rims to be coated. In general, count on about 1 teaspoon sugared or salted zest (½ teaspoon *each* zest and sugar or salt) per glass. Dip glasses in a liquid compatible with the drink (lime juice, tequila, and so on), then in sugared or salted zest. If possible, allow frosted glasses to dry for 1 hour, preferably in the freezer or refrigerator.

Other glass rim decorations include a coating of toasted coconut or sweetened cocoa powder.

FANS Use a sharp, pointed knife to cut the fruit or vegetable (such as a strawberry or radish) lengthwise into thin slices, slicing to within $\frac{1}{4}$ inch of the stem end. For strawberries, gently use your fingers to fan out the slices. Refrigerate radish fans in a bowl of ice water for 1 hour or until slices open up and fan out slightly. Blot dry with paper towel; refrigerate in a plastic bag until ready to use.

FLOWERS Edible flowers can either be floated on the surface of a drink or speared with a pick through the stem end. The first thing you need to know is that not all flowers are edible and if they aren't, they shouldn't touch anything you'll be drinking. Edible flowers (including chive blossoms, chrysanthemums, daisies, geraniums, jasmine, lavender, lilacs, marigolds, mimosa, nasturtiums, pansies, roses, and violets) are available at specialty produce markets and some supermarkets. If you're using something from your garden, make sure it isn't inherently poisonous and hasn't been sprayed with pesticide.

FROSTED GLASS RIMS *see* DECORATED GLASS RIMS

FRUIT, GENERAL Wash fruit that will be used unpeeled, like oranges, lemons, and limes. Keep fruits like bananas, peaches, and apples from darkening by coating the cut surface with lemon or lime juice; blot off excess. You can either dip the fruit into the juice, or use a pastry brush to coat the fruit. Remove the pits from fruit like cherries and apricots before using them as a garnish. Melon can be either peeled and cut into small wedges or chunks or cut into orbs with a melon baller, available at gourmet shops and some supermarkets.

ICE An easy, attractive garnish is decorative ice, which can add both eye-appeal and flavor. (For information on the importance of ice as a drink ingredient, *see* ICE, page 20.)

Decorative ice cubes: Place a small piece of fruit (cherry, grape, melon ball, pineapple chunk, raspberry, lemon or orange twist, etc.) or an edible flower or flower petal (*see* FLOWERS) in each section of an ice cube tray. Cover with cold water that has been boiled and cooled (which will produce clearer ice cubes than those made with plain tap water). Freeze until solid.

Frozen fruit "ice": Chunks of frozen fruit can be used just like ice, and can be eaten when they thaw in the drink. To make fruit ice, line a freezer-size baking sheet with plastic wrap. Cut peeled fruit (melon, pineapple, orange segments, plums, papaya) into large 1- to 1½-inch chunks or wedges. Brush the cut edges of fruit that darkens when exposed to air (like apples, peaches, and bananas) with lemon juice. Use fruit like strawberries and grapes whole. Place fruit on prepared baking sheet; freeze until solid, about 3 hours. Transfer fruit from baking sheet to a freezer bag; freeze for up to 3 months.

Flavored ice cubes: Create ice cubes with a nonalcoholic ingredient intrinsic to the drink. As flavored ice cubes melt, they infuse flavor into the drink. For example, you can make showy and delicious **watermelon cubes** with equal parts pureed seeded watermelon and cold water. Freeze in ice cube trays and add to drinks like Watermelon Margarita (page 122) or Watermelon Lemonade (page 144). You also can make lemonade cubes and add them to drinks like Not Yo' Momma's Lemonade (page 143). The amount of liquid needed depends on the size of the ice cube tray—most hold from 10 to 14 regular-size cubes. Don't use miniature ice cube trays—the tiny cubes melt too fast.

MINT Most markets sell mint in bunches, like a flower bouquet. To store, leave the bunch intact and place stems down in a glass of water. Cover with a plastic bag, securing it to the glass with a rubber band. Stored this way, mint should stay fresh for at least a week. To use as a garnish, pluck a mint sprig off the end of each stem. *See also* Mint Condition, page 132.

NUTMEG, FRESHLY GRATED A dusting of this spice makes a great garnish for creamy drinks like Big Easy Milk Punch (page 79) and Brandy Alexander (page 87). If all you've ever used is the ground nutmeg found on supermarket shelves, you're in for a treat. The freshly grated version has a lively, delicately warm and spicy flavor. Most supermarkets carry small jars of whole nutmegs (hard, grayish-brown, egg-shaped seeds about ¾ inch long) in the spice section. Kitchenware shops carry nutmeg graters and grinders.

OLIVES Stuffed olives make great garnishes for drinks like Martinis (page 124) and Bloody Marys (page 81). And many styles have special stuffings, from garlic to jalapeños. If you can't find such exotica, simply pluck the pimiento out of an olive and stuff it with whatever you like—almonds, cocktail onions, jalapeños, pickled garlic. For a change of pace, look for olives marinated in vermouth rather than brine—both styles are typically available in liquor stores and many supermarkets. Olives can either be dropped right into the drink (messy) or speared on a pick, which is easier to handle.

ONIONS, COCKTAIL Tiny cocktail onions turn a Martini (page 124) into a Gibson, and a Bloody Mary (page 81) into an onion lover's heaven. You'll find them in supermarkets and liquor stores—most are preserved in brine, some in vermouth.

SALTED (OR SUGARED) GLASS RIMS *see* DECO-
RATED GLASS RIMS

SCALLOPED EDGES Give lemons, oranges, cucumbers,
etc., a scalloped effect by using a CITRUS STRIPPER (page 36)
to cut evenly spaced channels lengthwise in the skin at about
$\frac{1}{2}$-inch intervals. When the fruit is sliced crosswise, the edges
look scalloped.

SLICES (WHEELS) Use a sharp knife to cut fruit (peeled
bananas, unpeeled citrus, etc.) crosswise into $\frac{1}{4}$-inch-thick
slices. Make a cut from the outer edge to the center of the slice
to create a slot for the fruit to straddle the glass rim. **For half-
slices,** cut the fruit crosswise in half, put the flat side down,
and cut into $\frac{1}{4}$-inch-thick slices. Create a slot by cutting from
the center to the inside edge of the peel to create a notch to
hook the fruit over the glass rim. **Foldover slices:** Fold a thin
slice of lemon, lime, or orange around a stemless maraschino
cherry and secure with a pick.

SPIRALS, CITRUS OR CUCUMBER Beginning at one
end of a lemon (or other citrus) or a cucumber, use a CITRUS
STRIPPER (page 36) to cut around and down the fruit, creating
a long, continuous spiral of skin.

STAR FRUIT Also known as a *carambola,* star fruit has a
thin, glossy golden skin and translucent, sweet-tart flesh the

same color. When star fruit is sliced crosswise, it has a strik-ing star shape, making it perfect for garnishing drinks. Wash the skin before slicing, but don't peel a star fruit.

TWISTS, GENERAL Thinly slice a fruit or vegetable (cu-cumber, orange, lemon, etc.); make one cut from the center to the edge. Twist the slice into a spiral (or S) shape. *See also* CITRUS TWISTS.

WEDGES, FRUIT Slice fruit lengthwise in half; cut each half lengthwise into quarters or eighths, depending on the size of the fruit. Make a cut from the center of the wedge to the inside edge of the peel to hook the fruit over the glass rim.

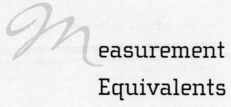

easurement Equivalents

MAE WEST ONCE SAID, "TOO MUCH OF A GOOD THING CAN BE wonderful." Right, but in a drink recipe, it can also ruin a pitcherful of drinks. So it's a good idea to use exact measurements with measuring cups and measuring spoons (page 39). You'll be glad you did.

EQUIVALENTS

3 teaspoons	1 tablespoon
1/2 tablespoon	1/4 fluid ounce; 1 1/2 teaspoons
1 tablespoon	1/2 fluid ounce; 3 teaspoons
2 tablespoons	1 fluid ounce; 1/8 cup
3 tablespoons	1 1/2 fluid ounces
4 tablespoons	2 fluid ounces; 1/4 cup
8 tablespoons	4 fluid ounces; 1/2 cup
1/8 cup	1 fluid ounce; 2 tablespoons

¼ cup	2 fluid ounces; 4 tablespoons
⅓ cup	Scant 3 ounces; 5 tablespoons plus 1 teaspoon
⅜ cup	3 ounces; ¼ cup plus 2 tablespoons
½ cup	4 fluid ounces; 8 tablespoons
⅔ cup	Scant 6 ounces; 10 tablespoons plus 2 teaspoons
¾ cup	6 fluid ounces; 12 tablespoons
1 cup	8 fluid ounces; ½ pint
2 cups	16 fluid ounces; 1 pint
3 cups	24 fluid ounces; 1½ pints
4 cups	32 fluid ounces; 1 quart
1 pint	16 fluid ounces; 2 cups
1 quart	32 fluid ounces; 2 pints; 4 cups
1 gallon	128 fluid ounces; 4 quarts; 8 pints; 16 cups

SPIRIT BOTTLE SIZES

Metric Measures	Fluid Ounces
100 ml.	3.4 ounces
200 ml.	6.8 ounces
500 ml.	16.9 ounces
750 ml.	25.4 ounces
1 liter	33.8 ounces
1.75 liters	59.2 ounces

WINE BOTTLE SIZES

Common Bottle Terminology	Metric Measure	Fluid Ounces
Miniature	100 ml.	3.4 ounces
Split	187 ml.	6.3 ounces
Half-bottle	375 ml.	12.7 ounces
500-milliliter	500 ml.	16.9 ounces
Bottle/750-milliliter	750 ml.	25.4 ounces
1 liter	1 liter	33.8 ounces

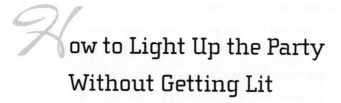

ow to Light Up the Party
Without Getting Lit

WHAT COULD BE BETTER THAN GETTING TOGETHER
with friends for a drink or two and something to
nibble on. No doubt about it, sharing good times
and laughter decreases stress and anxiety, makes
you smile, and leaves you feeling absolutely
wonderful. The trick is to have a great time while
drinking sensibly.

First of all, the good news is that according
to many scientists, moderate drinkers have lower
rates of coronary heart disease. (U.S. government
guidelines say moderate drinking is two average
drinks a day for a man, one for a woman.) The flip

side is that some people have a negative (even violent) physical or emotional reaction to alcohol.

How alcohol affects us depends on a complicated formula influenced by sex, weight, height, metabolism, body chemistry, and even race. For example, it's a physiological fact that women can't drink as much as men, in part because they lack a stomach and liver enzyme that men have (except for Japanese and Native American men). Alcohol breaks down four times faster in males than it does in females. Bummer!

Some people are sensitive to congeners (minute impurities) found in dark liquors like bourbon and Scotch. The purest distillate is vodka, followed by gin, which doesn't mean drinking too much of either won't make you sick. Studies have proven that mixing drinks (a Martini before dinner, wine with) really makes no difference—it's not *what* you drink but *how much*. One thing on which experts agree—too many sweet drinks (liqueurs or blended mixtures) virtually guarantee a hangover.

So let's get down to it—just how much is a drink? An "average drink" is equal to ½ ounce of pure 100 percent alcohol. But not all drinks are equal—here's how an average drink breaks down with spirits of varying alcohol levels:

- 1¼ ounces of 80-proof (40 percent alcohol) liquor, like rum and vodka

- 3 ounces of fortified wine, like sherry or port (about 16½ percent alcohol)
- 4 ounces of wine (12½ percent alcohol)
- 12 ounces of beer (4 percent alcohol)

Word to the wise: Drinks served in bars and restaurants can be over twice the size of an "average drink," and many beers contain more than 4 percent alcohol. The truth is that our bodies can only handle about one "average" drink per hour—it takes that long for the alcohol to transfer from stomach to bloodstream. And it takes at least four hours for the body to process alcohol. Bottom line: Knocking back three beers in an hour produces the same result as three Martinis—trouble.

One of the smartest ways to drink responsibly is simply to pace yourself. Drink slowly—guzzling is tacky, anyway. And down a glass of water for each drink. This is probably one of the most sensible things you can do because dehydration is the primary reason the morning after is so painful. If you think of it before you start partying, eat something (fruit, bread, and cheese are good choices). And take a vitamin C and a multi-B vitamin, the primary nutrients depleted by alcohol. Don't believe the myth about taking an aspirin before drinking. Rather than help, aspirin inhibits the alcohol from breaking down and can, in fact, cause from 40 to

100 percent more alcohol to be absorbed into your blood-stream.

Following are some tips for making parties fun for you and your guests:

- Serve mild to moderate drinks. Strong drinks should be served in smaller portions with lots of ice.

- Food slows the absorption of alcohol, so have plenty of it on hand. Choose foods high in fat (cheese), carbohydrates (bread products), and protein (meat or fish).

- Have plenty of cold, nonalcoholic beverages available—bottled water, fruit juices, Gatorade, milk, and soft drinks (though carbonation can slightly increase alcohol absorption). One reason drinking too much makes us feel so rotten is that we're dehydrated. The alcohol acts as a diuretic, pulling water out of our systems to flush out the toxins (along with myriad vitamins and nutrients). Encourage guests to have a glass of water or other liquor-free liquid for every drink they have.

- Tune into your guests—if someone's becoming intoxicated, get them to drink something non-alcoholic.

- If anyone's so far gone they can't drive, take their keys away and order a taxi, or have a sober guest drive them home. Caveat: In some states, a host is held legally responsible for any injuries or damage created by a guest who's been drinking in their home.

Drink and dance and laugh and lie,
    Love the reeling midnight through,
For tomorrow we shall die!
    (But, alas, we never do.)

—DOROTHY PARKER,
AMERICAN WRITER, WIT

Hangover Helpers

OKAY, SO THE PARTY'S OVER AND YOU *DIDN'T* PACE
yourself. In fact, you got downright drunk. So now
what? The room is spinning, your head is split-
ting, and your whole body feels lurchy—you'd like
to sober up a little before you hit the sack.

Sad, but true, there's no quick fix. Oh, there's
coffee, of course—everyone knows that works. *Not
bloody likely!* Caffeinated coffee's a diuretic and
actually aggravates the problem by increasing
dehydration—the primary reason your overboozed
body feels so rotten. And coffee doesn't in any
way speed sobering up. Neither will a cold

shower. Neither will a long walk. Time is all that works, guys, so you might as well lie back and relax as much as you can. But the following tips may just help assuage the morning after, so before you go to bed try the following:

- The primary way to get your mojo working is to re-hydrate your body. Drink more water—as much as you can. Better yet, drink a high-mineral sports beverage like Gatorade, which will help replenish electrolytes and get the water molecules flowing through your body. Don't worry about having to get up and go to the bathroom if you drink too much liquid. You're not going to sleep well anyway because, as the alcohol burns off and the body begins releasing adrenaline, your body will get fidgety and your temperature will increase slightly. You'll be restless and hot, tossing and turning. Get up, go to the bathroom, drink more water, and then go back to bed.
- If your stomach's okay, eat something to help absorb the alcohol and replenish lost nutrients—fruit (like bananas) or vegetables (potatoes are good). Some people swear by tomatoes.

- If your stomach's rocking and roiling, take an Alka-Seltzer or similar product.
- Take another multi-B vitamin and a vitamin C.

Still not feeling good the next morning? First of all, know that "the hair of the dog" will not cure a hangover. Oh, it might temporarily numb you, but then your body will have to start coping with the newly ingested alcohol, so why bother? Just drink more water or Gatorade, pop some more vitamins, go back to bed if you can, and eat something when your stomach will allow it.

Part Two

DIRECTORY OF DRINKS BY CATEGORY

POTENT CONCOCTIONS
(HIGH ALCOHOL)

Pitcher-Drink Recipes

*When I read about the evils of drinking,
I gave up reading.*

—HENNY YOUNGMAN,
AMERICAN COMEDIAN

*S*erve this one for dessert . . . actually, it's great any time you and your friends are feeling a little sinful. To keep the banana-slice garnishes from browning, brush them lightly with lemon or lime juice.

Makes twelve 5-ounce servings

> 2¹/₄ cups (18 ounces) dark rum
>
> 2¹/₄ cups (18 ounces) crème de banana
>
> 1¹/₂ cups (12 ounces) dark crème de cacao
>
> 1¹/₂ cups (12 ounces) heavy cream
>
> Garnish: 12 maraschino cherries with stems
>   and 12 banana slices

Combine all ingredients except garnish in a pitcher that holds at least 70 ounces; stir well. Cover and refrigerate at least 5 hours. Serve in 6-ounce cocktail glasses; garnish each serving by dropping in a cherry and hooking a banana slice over the rim.

variation

DOUBLE-TROUBLE B.S.: *Use 8-ounce cocktail glasses. Place a small scoop of vanilla or chocolate ice cream in each glass. If desired, drizzle with chocolate syrup.*

Top with drink mixture. Serve with spoons and short straws.

Starting with chilled ingredients shortens chilling time before a pitcher of drinks is ready to be served.

*B*ourbon is the spirit of choice for this drink in the Big Easy (New Orleans, for the those who don't know), but almost any liquor can be used, including brandy, gin, rum, and Scotch. Milk punch is perfect for everything from brunches to the morning after. This recipe is a rendition of one from my late friend Jamie Shannon, who was the longtime chef at New Orleans's Commander's Palace. Don't even think about using low-fat or nonfat milk—neither can deliver the smooth, silky texture this drink demands.

MAKES TWELVE 5.5-OUNCE SERVINGS

one 750-ml. bottle (25.4 ounces) bourbon,
    brandy, or other liquor
3 cups (24 ounces) cold whole milk
2 cups (16 ounces) cold half-and-half
1 cup superfine sugar
2 tablespoons (1 ounce) pure vanilla extract
GARNISH: Freshly grated nutmeg

Combine all ingredients except garnish in a pitcher that holds at least 80 ounces; stir well to dissolve sugar. Cover

and refrigerate at least 4 hours. Serve in 6-ounce old-fashioned glasses, with or without ice cubes. Garnish by *lightly* sprinkling nutmeg on each serving.

variation

LATTE MILK PUNCH: *Dissolve 3 tablespoons instant espresso powder (or ¼ cup regular instant coffee) in 2 tablespoons very hot water. Add to remaining ingredients before chilling. Garnish with a dusting of cocoa powder or cocoa mix.*

merica's most popular alcoholic drink is as multifaceted as a diamond and perfect for parties, no matter what time of day. Bloody Marys can range from mild to mouth-searing, and be garnished with everything from celery to pickled okra. You'll notice that this pitcher version calls for a small amount of water. That's necessary because the traditional Bloody Mary is made by vigorously shaking the ingredients with ice, which slightly dilutes the mix with water and produces the perfect texture. Liven things up and let everyone do their own thing with a build-your-own Bloody Mary bar (see page 83).

MAKES TEN 6.5-OUNCE SERVINGS

5 cups (40 ounces) tomato juice or V-8 juice

2 cups (16 ounces) vodka

$^2/_3$ cup (scant 6 ounces) water

$^1/_2$ cup (4 ounces) fresh lemon juice

$2^1/_2$ teaspoons Worcestershire sauce

$1^1/_2$ to 2 teaspoons Tabasco sauce or other hot sauce

$1^1/_2$ to 2 teaspoons horseradish (optional)

$^1/_2$ teaspoon celery salt

$^1/_2$ teaspoon black pepper

Salt to taste

GARNISH: 10 celery stalks with leaves, lemon
wedges, cherry tomatoes, or all three

Combine all ingredients except garnish in a pitcher that
holds at least 80 ounces; stir well. Can be served immediately or covered and refrigerated until ready to serve. Fill
10- to 12-ounce glasses (any shape) two-thirds full with
ice cubes. Add drink mixture; garnish as desired (spear
lemon wedge and tomato together on a cocktail pick).

variations

BLOODY BREW: *Reduce tomato juice to 3$^1/_2$ cups, and
vodka to 1 cup; omit water. Just before serving,
slowly add two 12-ounce bottles of icy-cold beer
(generally, the darker, the more full-flavored), tilting the pitcher and pouring onto the pitcher's side to
retain as much effervescence as possible. Stir gently
to combine.*

BLOODY BULL: *Substitute 2$^1/_2$ cups (20 ounces) beef broth
or beef bouillon for 2$^1/_2$ cups of the tomato juice.*

BLOODY CAESAR: *Substitute Clamato juice for the tomato
juice.*

BLOODY HELL: *Substitute 1 cup tequila for 1 cup of the
vodka; increase Tabasco to 1$^1/_2$ tablespoons. Garnish
each serving with a small jalapeño pepper.*

BLOODY MARIA: *Substitute tequila for the vodka and lime*

juice for the lemon juice; garnish each serving with a lime wedge.

BLOODY SUNRISE: *Reduce tomato juice to 3 cups (24 ounces), add 3 cups (24 ounces) fresh orange juice, and omit water. Garnish each serving with half an orange slice.*

JAZZY MARY: *Substitute flavored vodka (pepper, lemon, orange, etc.) for regular vodka.*

RED RUMBA: *Substitute gold rum for the vodka and lime juice for the lemon juice; garnish each serving with a lime wedge.*

RED SNAPPER: *Substitute gin for the vodka.*

VIRGIN MARY: *Omit vodka; increase tomato juice to 6½ cups and water to 1 cup.*

BLOODY
MARY BAR

Everyone's personality is different . . . so is their taste in Bloody Marys. Let your guests get into the action by building their own drink. Set everything out on the bar or countertop and let 'em have at it. Here's what you need:

- Pitcher or two of Bloody Marys

- Tall glasses, double old-fashioned glasses, or anything else you have

- Bucket of ice (with ice tongs or ice scoop)

- Iced-tea spoons for stirring

- **Tabasco (red or green) or other hot sauce**

- **Horseradish—regular or wasabi (Japanese horse-radish)**

- **Salt and pepper**

- **Garnishes (any or all)**

> Sticks of celery, carrot, cucumber, and red and green pepper
>
> Scallions (*see also* scallion brushes, page 44)
>
> Large stuffed olives
>
> Cherry tomatoes
>
> Cornichons or dill pickle spears
>
> Pickled okra
>
> Lemon and lime wedges
>
> Jalapeño peppers
>
> Jicama slices
>
> Sprigs of mint, rosemary, parsley, or oregano
>
> Dilled string beans
>
> Baby corn
>
> Minced fresh onion and/or garlic (or powdered garlic and onion)

*T*he flavor of this drink is reminiscent of those cinnamon candied apples many of us loved as children. If you have time, make this at least an hour in advance so the apples have time to soak up some of the liquid. For a lighter, less sweet version, try the fizzy variation.

MAKES TWELVE 5.75-OUNCE SERVINGS

5 cups (40 ounces) apple juice

2 cups (16 ounces) Calvados or other apple brandy

3/4 cup (6 ounces) Goldschläger or other cinnamon schnapps

1/2 cup (4 ounces) fresh lemon juice

1/3 cup (scant 3 ounces) Tuaca

1 large apple cut into 10 wedges

Combine all ingredients in a pitcher that holds at least 80 ounces; stir well. Can be served immediately or covered and refrigerated until ready to serve. Fill 10-ounce wineglasses almost full with crushed ice. Add drink mixture, along with an apple wedge; serve with a straw.

BRANDIED APPLE FIZZ: *Use a pitcher that holds at least
100 ounces. Just before serving, slowly add 2½ cups
(20 ounces) icy-cold lemon-flavored sparkling
water, tilting the pitcher and pouring onto the
pitcher's side to retain as much effervescence as
possible. Stir gently to combine. Serve in 12-ounce
tall glasses filled two-thirds full with ice cubes.*

*Brandy, n. A cordial composed of one part
thunder-and-lightning, one part remorse,
two parts bloody murder, one part
death-hell-and-the-grave and four parts
clarified Satan.*

—AMBROSE BIERCE,
AMERICAN SATIRIST,
THE DEVIL'S DICTIONARY

*C*alled "Andy Bralexander" by those who've had too many, this innocent-tasting after-dinner drink has endless flavor permutations. It can be served either UP in a cocktail glass or ON THE ROCKS in an old-fashioned glass. As always, if you serve a drink without ice, it's nice to have the glasses chilled.

MAKES TWELVE 4-OUNCE SERVINGS

2 cups (16 ounces) brandy

2 cups (16 ounces) white crème de cacao

2 cups (16 ounces) half-and-half or heavy cream

$1/2$ cup (4 ounces) cold water

GARNISH: Freshly grated nutmeg

Combine all ingredients except garnish in a pitcher that holds at least 50 ounces; stir well. If you're going to serve these drinks sans ice in 5-ounce cocktail glasses, cover and refrigerate at least 4 hours. To serve them immediately, fill 6-ounce old-fashioned glasses two-thirds full with ice cubes. Add drink mixture; *lightly* sprinkle each serving with nutmeg.

ALEXANDER MINT: *Use dark crème de cacao and reduce it to 1 cup (8 ounces); add ½ cup (4 ounces) white or green crème de menthe. Garnish each serving with a chocolate-covered mint, slit halfway to the middle and perched on the glass rim.*

BRANDY ALEXANDER FREEZE: *Cover pitcher of drink mixture; freeze overnight. Briskly stir just before serving.*

CLASSIC ALEXANDER: *Substitute gin for the brandy.*

DREAMY ALEXANDER: *Reduce crème de cacao to ¾ cup (6 ounces) and add ¾ cup (6 ounces) Cointreau. Garnish each serving with half an orange slice.*

GRASSHOPPER: *Substitute green crème de menthe for the brandy.*

MOCHA ALEXANDER: *Reduce crème de cacao to ¾ cup (6 ounces) and add ¾ cup (6 ounces) Kahlúa or other coffee-flavored liqueur. Garnish each serving with a sprinkle of cocoa powder or cocoa mix.*

RUMMY ALEXANDER: *Substitute dark rum for the brandy.*

WICKED ALEXANDER: *Substitute 1 pint slightly softened premium vanilla ice cream for the half-and-half or cream; omit water. In a blender, process the brandy, crème de cacao, and ice cream until smooth. Serve immediately in 5-ounce cocktail glasses.*

CAIPIRINHA [KUY-per-REEN-yah]

*O*n a sweltering day, the limey sweet-tart taste of Brazil's national drink is downright addictive. The Caipirinha's smooth flavor belies its potency, for this seductive sipper is made with CACHAÇA *(page 11),* Brazil's sugarcane firewater. Caipirinhas are classically made either by muddling lime wedges and sugar in a shaker, adding cachaça and ice, and shaking like crazy, or by muddling lime and sugar in a glass, then topping with crushed ice and cachaça. Naturally, for this pitcher-drink version, we're doing it differently—squeezing the limes. And for a more complex flavor, I use cane syrup instead of sugar, a trick learned from my pal Cindy Pawlcyn, the Napa Valley restaurateur icon (Mustards Grill, Miramonte, and previously Fog City Diner and others). Less of the pure cane syrup is needed because it's more concentrated than the mock cane syrup. If you don't use either store-bought or homemade syrup (big mistake!), substitute ²/₃ to 1¹/₃ cups superfine sugar, stirring well to dissolve. One last thing: Don't forget to suck on the lime wedges that've soaked for hours in the cachaça mixture—they're fully loaded and incredibly refreshing.

10 medium to large limes, washed and
    quartered

2¹/₂ cups (20 ounces) cachaça

1 cup (8 ounces) pure cane syrup or 1¹/₄ cups
    (10 ounces) Mock Cane Syrup (*see follow-*
    ing recipe)

¹/₃ cup (scant 3 ounces) water

If you're making the Mock Cane Syrup, do it first. Squeeze
the juice from the lime quarters into a pitcher that holds at
least 50 ounces; drop the squeezed fruit into the pitcher as
well. Don't knock yourself out to extract all of the lime
juice—a brief squeeze will do (*see* Squeeze Play, page 113).
Add cachaça, cane syrup, and water; stir briskly. Cover and
refrigerate at least 4 hours. Fill 12-ounce double old-
fashioned glasses almost full with crushed ice. Add 3 to 4 of
the squeezed lime quarters to each glass; top with drink
mixture. Serve with straws, if desired.

*I always keep a bottle of stimulant handy in
case I see a snake—which I also keep handy.*

— W. C. FIELDS,
AMERICAN COMEDIAN, ACTOR

3/4 cup (6 ounces) water

2/3 cup packed light brown sugar

1/3 cup superfine sugar

1 teaspoon dark molasses

In a small saucepan, heat water just until simmering. Remove from heat; add sugars and molasses, stirring until dissolved. If you're making this at the last minute and don't have time to let it cool: Combine 1/4 cup of the water with the brown sugar. Heat until water bubbles. Remove from heat and stir until sugar dissolves. Add remaining 1/2 cup cold water, superfine sugar, and molasses; stir to dissolve sugar.

variations

CAIPIRISSIMA: *Substitute rum for the cachaça.*
CAIPIROSKA: *Substitute vodka for the cachaça.*

*C*ream of coconut has a tendency to separate in the can. Before measuring, either stir it well or toss it into a blender and process at medium speed until smooth.

3¼ cups (26 ounces) cream of coconut

3¼ cups (26 ounces) fresh lime juice

1½ cups (12 ounces) dark rum

1 cup (8 ounces) Malibu coconut rum

GARNISH: 12 lime slices

Combine all ingredients except garnish in a pitcher that holds at least 80 ounces; stir well. Can be served immediately or covered and refrigerated until ready to serve. Fill 10-ounce tall glasses three-quarters full with crushed ice; add drink mixture. Garnish each serving with a lime slice, hooking over the glass rim; serve with a straw.

Recipes like the Cosmopolitan (page 94) and the Martini (page 124) have a small amount of water in the ingredients list. No, it's not a mistake, and, no, you shouldn't leave it out thinking that it'll dilute the drink. There's a plan here. You see, in recipes where the ingredients are typically shaken with ice for a single-drink preparation, the ice melts slightly, adding water to the mix and contributing just the right texture. So, at least in this case, water retention is a good thing.

COSMOPOLITAN

*N*icknamed the "stealth Martini" for its innocent appearance and spirited kick, the classic Cosmopolitan is one of today's most popular drinks. Frosting the glass rims (see DECORATED GLASS RIMS, *page 47*) with sugared lime zest is not only colorful, but also adds a hit of flavor that's decidedly addictive. Speaking of lime, Cosmo aficionados shudder at the thought of using Rose's or other sweetened lime juice, which tastes about as much like the real thing as figs do trout. Cosmopolitans are meant to be lively fusions of liquor and juice, unadulterated by added sugar. If you don't want to buy a jug of cranberry juice, look for the sweetened liquid concentrate, which allows you to make as much as you want as you need it.

MAKES TWELVE 5-OUNCE SERVINGS

3 cups (24 ounces) vodka

1½ cups (12 ounces) Cointreau

1½ cups (12 ounces) cranberry juice

¾ cup (6 ounces) fresh lime juice

½ cup (4 ounces) water

GARNISH: 12 lime slices

If desired, frost the rims of 6-ounce cocktail glasses by moistening with a little cranberry or lime juice, then dipping the rim into Sugared Citrus Zest (see Zested Glass Rim, page 47) or simply into granulated sugar. Glasses may be frosted ahead of time; chill in the refrigerator if there's room. Combine all ingredients except garnish in a pitcher that holds at least 65 ounces; stir well. Cover and refrigerate at least 4 hours, or freeze for 2 hours. Pour drink mixture into prepared glasses; garnish each serving with a lime slice, hooking it over the glass rim.

variation

 UNCORRUPTED COSMO: *Omit vodka, Cointreau, and water. Use the following: 3 cups (24 ounces) Rose's Non-Alcoholic Triple Sec, 3 cups (24 ounces) cranberry juice, and 1½ cups (12 ounces) fresh lime juice.*

The original Daiquiri (invented in Cuba in 1896 by American mining engineer Jennings Cox) was shaken with ice and served up, like a Martini. Today it's often served over ice and frequently laced with pureed fruit. Sugar-frosting the glass rim is optional (see DECORATED GLASS RIMS, page 47).

makes ten 4-ounce servings

one 750-ml. bottle (25.4 ounces) light rum
1½ cups (12 ounces) fresh lime juice
¾ cup (6 ounces) water
¼ to ⅓ cup superfine sugar
garnish: 10 lime slices

Combine all ingredients except garnish in a pitcher that holds at least 55 ounces; stir well to dissolve sugar. Cover and refrigerate at least 4 hours. Serve in 6-ounce cocktail glasses; garnish each serving with a lime slice, hooking it over the glass rim.

variations

BANANA DAIQUIRI *(makes ten 6.5-ounce servings): Use a pitcher that holds at least 80 ounces. Increase lime*

juice to 3 cups (24 ounces), omit water, and add
¾ cup (6 ounces) crème de banana and 1½ cups (12
ounces) ripe banana puree. Cover and refrigerate at
least 4 hours. **For Frozen Banana Daiquiris:** Freeze
overnight; stir well just before serving. Serve in
7-ounce cocktail glasses; garnish each serving with
a banana slice.

BLUE MOON DAIQUIRI: Use a pitcher that holds 60
ounces. Add ¾ cup (6 ounces) parfait amour or blue
curaçao.

DAIQUIRI DE AGAVE: Substitute silver tequila for the rum.

DERBY DAIQUIRI: Use a pitcher that holds 60 ounces. Omit
water and add 1½ cups (12 ounces) fresh orange juice
(for added orange flavor, use ½ cup frozen orange
juice concentrate and enough water to equal 1½
cups). If desired, add ¼ teaspoon orange flower
water. Garnish each serving with an orange slice.

FROZEN DAIQUIRI: Place Daiquiri mixture in the freezer
overnight; stir just before serving.

STRAWBERRY DAIQUIRI (makes twelve 7-ounce servings):
Use a 100-ounce pitcher; omit water. Add 3 pints
strawberries, trimmed, washed, and pureed; strain
if desired. Just before serving, stir vigorously. Serve
in 8-ounce wine or cocktail glasses; garnish each
serving with a whole strawberry, slit from the base
almost to the leaves and hooked over the glass rim.

*T*his colorful tiki drink slides down sweet and
easy, but it's plenty potent. If you really want to go
tropical, adorn these drinks with little paper umbrellas,
available in liquor, party, and novelty stores.

MAKES TWELVE 7-OUNCE SERVINGS

2½ cups (20 ounces) water

2 cups (16 ounces) silver tequila

1¾ cups (14 ounces) blue curaçao

1½ cups (12 ounces) coconut milk

1¼ cups (10 ounces) crème de banana

¾ cup (6 ounces) thawed frozen lemonade
    concentrate

⅔ cup (scant 6 ounces) Rose's Lime Juice

GARNISH: 10 orange slices and 10 maraschino
    cherries

Combine all ingredients except garnish in a pitcher that
holds at least 95 ounces; stir well. Can be served immediately or covered and refrigerated until ready to serve. Fill
12-ounce tall glasses or wineglasses two-thirds full with
ice cubes. Add drink mixture; garnish each serving with an
orange slice and cherry skewered on a cocktail pick.

JAMAICAN DÉJÀ BLUE: *Substitute gold rum for the tequila.*

You can't drown yourself in drink.
I've tried . . . you float.

—JOHN BARRYMORE,
AMERICAN ACTOR

This drink is perfect for daytime festivities, from brunches to lunches, to weddings . . . but then again, it's also a great apéritif. The blend of passion fruit, black raspberry, and a kiss of ginger is intensely exotic and just the thing for special occasions. If you don't have tall champagne flutes, use white wine glasses.

MAKES TWELVE 6-OUNCE SERVINGS

2 cups (16 ounces) Alizé Gold Passion liqueur or
    other passion fruit liqueur
1/2 cup (4 ounces) Chambord
1/4 cup (2 ounces) Canton Delicate Ginger
    Liqueur
two 750-ml. bottles (50.8 ounces) icy-cold brut
    champagne
GARNISH: 12 fresh raspberries plus 12 small
    edible flowers (optional)

Combine first three ingredients in a pitcher that holds at least 80 ounces; stir well. Cover and refrigerate at least 4 hours. Just before serving, slowly add champagne, tilting the pitcher and pouring onto the pitcher's side to retain as much effervescence as possible. Stir gently to combine.

Pour into 7-ounce flutes or wineglasses; drop a raspberry into each serving. If desired, float an edible flower (page 48) in each serving.

If you're given Champagne at lunch,
there's a catch somewhere.

—LORD LYONS,
BRITISH ARISTOCRAT

The colder this drink, the more seductively satiny its texture. If you have room, leave the pitcher in the freezer for a couple of hours. This is a lovely afternoon or après-dinner sipper. For a lighter drink, omit the half-and-half and increase the water to 1½ cups (12 ounces).

1½ cups (12 ounces) gin

1½ cups (12 ounces) Cointreau

¾ cup (6 ounces) Absente or Pernod

¾ cup (6 ounces) half-and-half

¾ cup (6 ounces) water

¼ cup (2 ounces) crème de menthe

garnish: 12 orange slices

Combine all ingredients except garnish in a 50-ounce pitcher. Cover and refrigerate at least 4 hours. Serve in 5-ounce cocktail glasses; garnish each serving with an orange slice, hooking it over the rim of the glass.

TROPICAL GREEN GENIE: *Substitute 1½ cups (12 ounces) coconut milk (not cream of coconut) for the half-and-half and water.*

I'd hate to be a teetotaler. Imagine getting up in the morning and knowing that's as good as you're going to feel all day.

—DEAN MARTIN,
AMERICAN SINGER, ACTOR

*B*e careful of this one—it's sweetly fruity but can hit you like a category-five hurricane! It was born in New Orleans's French Quarter at Pat O'Brien's bar and has become so popular that there's now a Pat O'Brien's Hurricane mix to which one simply adds rum and water. Even if you can find the mix, fresh is better in my book. Passion fruit juice (also called passion fruit nectar) can be found in many supermarkets and natural food stores, as well as most liquor stores. Many glassware stores carry special hurricane glasses (shaped like a hurricane lamp), but any tall glass will do.

Makes ten 7.5-ounce servings

> 2½ cups (20 ounces) passion fruit juice or
> nectar
> 2 cups (16 ounces) dark rum
> 1¾ cups (14 ounces) light rum
> 1¾ cups (14 ounces) fresh orange juice
> 1¼ cups (10 ounces) fresh lime juice
> 3½ tablespoons (1¾ ounces) grenadine syrup
> Garnish: 10 maraschino cherries and
> 10 orange slices

Combine all ingredients except garnish in a pitcher that holds at least 85 ounces; stir well. Can be served immediately or covered and refrigerated until ready to serve. Fill 12-ounce tall glasses two-thirds full with ice cubes. Add drink mixture; garnish each serving with a cherry and orange slice skewered on a cocktail pick.

variation

SOUTHERN HURRICANE: *Substitute Southern Comfort for the light rum.*

If you were to ask me if I'd ever had the bad luck to miss my daily cocktail, I'd have to say that I doubt it; where certain things are concerned, I plan ahead.

—LUIS BUÑUEL,
SPANISH FILMMAKER

he Kamikaze began as a shooter, though today it's just as often served UP *in a cocktail glass or* ON THE ROCKS *in an old-fashioned glass. Some recipes use Rose's Lime Juice, but not mine—I like the hit of fresh lime juice no bottled version can deliver.*

MAKES TWELVE 5-OUNCE SERVINGS

2¼ cups (18 ounces) vodka

2¼ cups (18 ounces) triple sec

2¼ cups (18 ounces) fresh lime juice

²/₃ cup (scant 6 ounces) water

Combine all ingredients in a pitcher that holds at least 70 ounces; stir well. If you're going to serve these drinks sans ice in 6-ounce cocktail glasses, cover and refrigerate at least 4 hours. To serve them immediately, fill 8-ounce old-fashioned glasses two-thirds full with ice cubes; add drink mixture.

VARIATIONS

BLUE KAMIKAZE: *Substitute blue curaçao for the triple sec.*

KAMIKAZE FIZZ *(makes twelve 6.5-ounce servings):* Use a pitcher that holds at least 90 ounces; omit water. Just *before serving, slowly add 3 cups (24 ounces) icy-cold seltzer water or club soda, tilting the pitcher and pouring onto the pitcher's side to retain as much effervescence as possible. Stir gently to combine. Fill 10-ounce tall glasses two-thirds full with ice cubes; add drink mixture.*

SOUTHERN KAMIKAZE: *Substitute Southern Comfort for the triple sec.*

May you be in heaven half an hour before the devil knows you're dead.

—TRADITIONAL IRISH TOAST

*T*here is also a Key Lime Pie shooter, but this cocktail is definitely for slow sipping. Flavorwise, it's like the pie without the crust, which means fewer calories (Sharon's motto: Rationalization is good). Sorry to say, there's no real substitute for Licor 43, though Tuaca may be used in a pinch. The combination of the cream and the acid in the limes causes this drink to separate slightly, but a brief whirl in a blender (in two batches) will help. Remember: The lighter the cream, the more separation—definitely don't try to use milk.

makes ten 5-ounce servings

2½ cups (20 ounces) Licor 43

1¼ cups (10 ounces) light rum

1¼ cups (10 ounces) heavy cream or
    half-and-half

⅔ cup (scant 6 ounces) Rose's Lime Juice

⅔ cup (scant 6 ounces) water

1½ tablespoons (¾ ounce) fresh lime juice

garnish: 10 cherry twists (using lime peel)
    (page 45) or 10 lime slices

Combine all ingredients except garnish in a 65-ounce pitcher. Cover and refrigerate at least 4 hours. If desired, dip glass rims into lime juice, then into sugared lime zest (see DECORATED GLASS RIMS, page 47). Serve in 6-ounce cocktail glasses; garnish each serving with a cherry twist, or a lime slice hooked over the glass rim.

It is an odd but universally held opinion that anyone who doesn't drink must be an alcoholic.

— P. J. O'ROURKE,
AMERICAN WIT, AUTHOR

*L*emon Drops go down so easily they're danger-
ous. Intensify the citrus flavor by using a lemon-
flavored vodka, such as Absolut Citron.

> 4 cups (32 ounces) vodka
>
> 2/3 cup (scant 6 ounces) water
>
> 2/3 cup (scant 6 ounces) fresh lemon juice
>
> 2/3 cup superfine sugar
>
> garnish: 10 lemon slices or wedges

Combine all ingredients except garnish in a pitcher that
holds at least 55 ounces; stir vigorously to dissolve sugar.
Cover and refrigerate at least 4 hours. Frost the rims of
5-ounce cocktail glasses by moistening with a little lemon
juice or water, then dipping rim into granulated sugar (see
DECORATED GLASS RIMS, page 47). If you have room in your
freezer, chill the glasses for an hour before serving. Pour
drink mixture into prepared glasses; garnish each serving
with lemon slice or wedge, hooked over the glass rim.

variations

BRAZILIAN LIME DROP: *Substitute cachaça for the vodka,
fresh lime juice for the lemon juice, and packed light*

brown sugar for the superfine sugar. Stir vigorously to dissolve brown sugar.

LIME DROP: *Substitute fresh lime juice for the lemon juice.*

LIVELY LEMON DROP: *Substitute pepper-flavored vodka (such as Absolut Peppar) for the regular vodka.*

ORANGE DROP: *Substitute orange-flavored vodka for the regular vodka and 1/8 cup (1 ounce) frozen orange juice concentrate plus 1/2 cup (4 ounces) water for the lemon juice. Garnish each serving with an orange slice.*

SASSY LEMON DROP: *Add 1/2 to 3/4 teaspoon Tabasco sauce.*

ubstituting Alizé Red liqueur for the Alizé Gold (page 9) transforms this drink's color and flavor—it's different, but still delicious. Liven up the party by giving each drink a FLOAT *(page 17) of Demerara rum.*

MAKES TWELVE 7-OUNCE SERVINGS

one 750-ml. bottle (25.4 ounces) light or gold rum

1½ cups (12 ounces) Alizé Gold or other passion
    fruit liqueur

1½ cups (12 ounces) fresh orange juice

1 cup (8 ounces) fresh lime juice

¼ cup (2 ounces) Demerara (151-proof) rum
    (optional)

5 cups crushed ice

GARNISH: 12 star fruit or orange slices

Combine all ingredients except crushed ice and garnish in a pitcher that holds at least 100 ounces; stir well. Cover and refrigerate at least 4 hours. Just before serving, add crushed ice and stir vigorously. Pour into 8-ounce cocktail glasses. If desired, float a teaspoon of 151-proof rum on the surface of each drink. Garnish each serving with a star fruit slice or orange slice, hooking it over the glass rim.

LIQUADO O₂: *Substitute gold tequila for the rum; garnish with lime slices.*

squeeze
play

Tips for Maximum Juice from Lemons, Limes, and Oranges

- The juiciest lemons (and other citrus) are those heavy for their size.

- Room-temperature fruit yields more juice than cold fruit.

- Soften fruit to loosen juice by pressing down on it with your palm and rolling it around on the countertop several times.

- Zapping it will warm refrigerated fruit and help free up the juice. Use a fork to prick the skin in several places (don't go all the way through to the flesh), then microwave on high for about 15 seconds. Let stand 2 minutes before rolling the fruit between your palm and the countertop.

- Only need a little juice? Soften the fruit, then insert a CITRUS SPOUT (page 36) and squeeze out just what you need.

- Cover and refrigerate leftover fresh-squeezed citrus juice for up to 5 days.

he only resemblance this drink has to iced tea is color. Whereas the original recipe uses silver tequila and light rum, my rendition ups the ante with gold tequila and Captain Morgan Original Spiced Rum. And instead of using sweet-and-sour mix (why go out and buy a bottle?), we're creating our own with a water–lemon juice–sugar combo. By the way, the variation is for all my Texas friends who're hooked on Dr Pepper, invented in 1885 in Waco, Texas.

MAKES TEN 6-OUNCE SERVINGS

$2/3$ cup (scant 6 ounces) gold tequila

$2/3$ cup (scant 6 ounces) spiced rum

$2/3$ cup (scant 6 ounces) vodka

$2/3$ cup (scant 6 ounces) gin

$2/3$ cup (scant 6 ounces) triple sec

1 cup (8 ounces) water

$1/2$ cup (4 ounces) fresh lemon juice

$1/4$ cup superfine sugar

$2^1/2$ cups (20 ounces) icy-cold cola

GARNISH: 10 lemon wedges or slices

Combine all ingredients except cola and garnish in a pitcher that holds at least 75 ounces. Can be served immediately or covered and refrigerated until ready to serve. Just before serving, slowly add cola, tilting the pitcher and pouring onto the pitcher's side to retain as much effervescence as possible. Stir gently to combine. Fill 10-ounce tall glasses three-quarters full with ice cubes. Add drink mixture; garnish each serving with a lemon wedge or slice, hooking it over the glass rim.

variation

TEXAS ICED TEA: *Substitute icy cold Dr Pepper for the cola.*

FUGGEDABOUDIT!

Don't even think about using the lemon or lime juice found in bottles or little plastic fruits on supermarket shelves. It often has a nasty flavor that in no way resembles freshly squeezed juice. If you can't find fresh lemons (or just don't want to squeeze them), Minute Maid's frozen lemon juice is an acceptable substitute. There's no such product available for fresh lime juice.

*H*istory tells us that the Mai Tai (Tahitian for "the very best") was created in 1944 by Victor Bergeron at his original Trader Vic's restaurant in Oakland, California. The following proportions follow Trader Vic's original recipe except that rather than have you make or buy sugar syrup, we're doing it the easy pitcher-drink way with water and sugar. If you want to be authentic, use Jamaican rum and don't tart up the drink with a lot of fruit.

MAKES TWELVE 5.25-OUNCE SERVINGS

4 cups (32 ounces) gold rum

1½ cups (12 ounces) fresh lime juice

1 cup (8 ounces) orange curaçao

1 cup (8 ounces) orgeat syrup

⅓ cup (scant 3 ounces) water

⅔ cup superfine sugar

GARNISH: 12 mint sprigs

Combine all ingredients except garnish in a pitcher that holds at least 75 ounces; stir well to dissolve sugar. Can be served immediately, or covered and refrigerated until ready to serve. Fill 8-ounce old-fashioned glasses with crushed ice; add drink mixture. Garnish each serving with a mint sprig; serve with a straw.

I think a man ought to get drunk at least twice a year just on principle, so he won't let himself get snotty about it.

—RAYMOND CHANDLER, AMERICAN AUTHOR

This classic was created in New York City in the late 1800s by a bartender at the Manhattan Club. Rye is the classic spirit used, though today you'll find "Manhattans" made with everything from bourbon to tequila. Undisputable, however, is that a Manhattan must contain bitters, without which it would simply be another drink. Although Manhattans are traditionally served UP *in cocktail glasses, they may also be served* ON THE ROCKS *in old-fashioned glasses.*

MAKES TWELVE 3.5-OUNCE SERVINGS

3 cups (24 ounces) rye, bourbon, or blended
   whiskey
1½ cups (12 ounces) sweet vermouth
¾ to 1 teaspoon Angostura bitters
⅔ cup (scant 6 ounces) water
GARNISH: 12 maraschino cherries with stems

Combine all ingredients except garnish in a pitcher that holds at least 55 ounces; stir well. Cover and refrigerate at least 4 hours. Serve in 5-ounce cocktail glasses; garnish each serving with a cherry.

DRY MANHATTAN: *Substitute dry vermouth for the sweet vermouth; garnish each serving with a lemon twist.*

MEXICAN MANHATTAN: *Substitute añejo tequila for the rye; garnish each serving with an orange twist.*

PERFECT MANHATTAN: *Substitute ¾ cup (6 ounces) dry vermouth for ¾ cup (6 ounces) of the sweet vermouth.*

ROB ROY: *Substitute Scotch for the rye.*

Lead me not into temptation;
I can find the way myself.

—RITA MAE BROWN,
AMERICAN AUTHOR

*F or a classic Margarita, the ingredients are typi-
cally shaken with ice (the melting water from the ice
creates a silky-smooth texture), then strained and
served* UP *in a stemmed glass—anything from a cocktail
glass, to a wineglass, to the characteristic "Margarita"
glass. Truth is, Margaritas can be served in almost any
vessel (including in a squat old-fashioned glass), and
are equally delicious served* ON THE ROCKS. *If you don't
have time to chill this pitcher drink, serve it over ice
cubes. Traditionally, Mexican-style Margaritas are
made with silver tequila, but any tequila can be used,
depending on your taste (see* TEQUILA, *page 29).*

Makes Ten 6-ounce servings

one 750-ml. bottle (25.4 ounces) silver tequila

2 cups (16 ounces) triple sec

1½ cups (12 ounces) fresh lime juice

1 cup (8 ounces) water

Garnish: 10 lime slices (optional)

**Moisten the rims of ten 8-ounce glasses (12-ounce glasses
if serving over ice cubes) with a little lime juice, then dip**

rim into salt, or use salted citrus zest (*see* DECORATED GLASS RIMS, **page 47**). Put glasses in the fridge if you have room. Combine all ingredients except garnish in a pitcher that holds at least 70 ounces; stir well. Cover and refrigerate at least 4 hours. Pour drink mixture into prepared glasses; if desired, garnish each serving with a lime slice hooked over the glass rim.

v a r i a t i o n s

BLUE MARGARITA: *Substitute blue curaçao for the triple sec.*

COCORITA: *If desired, coat glass rims with toasted coconut* (see **DECORATED GLASS RIMS**, *page 47). Omit triple sec and water; add 1 cup (8 ounces) cream of coconut and 2 cups (16 ounces) pineapple juice.*

COSMORITA *(makes ten 7.5-ounce servings): Use an 85-ounce pitcher. Omit water; add 2 cups (16 ounces) cranberry juice.*

FROZEN MARGARITA: *Cover any pitcher of Margaritas and place in freezer overnight; stir just before serving. Fruit Margaritas should be removed from the freezer 20 to 30 minutes ahead of time to allow for the extra solids to thaw.*

FRUIT MARGARITA *(makes about ten 9-ounce servings): Use a pitcher that holds at least 100 ounces and 10-ounce glasses (12-ounce if serving over ice). Puree 6 rounded cups strawberries or chopped, peeled kiwi, mango, papaya, peaches, pineapple, and so on. Pour into pitcher; add other ingredients except water. Cover and refrigerate at least 4 hours. Stir just before* serving; garnish each serving with a piece of the fruit used in the ingredients.

MARGARITA DEL SOL: *Omit water. Substitute Licor 43 for the triple sec, reduce lime juice to 1 cup (8 ounces), and add 1½ cups (12 ounces) fresh orange juice. Garnish each serving with an orange slice.*

MEZCALITA: *Substitute mezcal for tequila and add 2 teaspoons bitters.*

MIGHTY MELONITA *(makes about ten 9-ounce servings): Use a pitcher that holds at least 100 ounces and 10-ounce glasses (12-ounce if serving over ice). Substitute Midori or other melon-flavored liqueur for the triple sec; omit water. Puree 6 rounded cups honeydew, cantaloupe, or other melon; stir into other ingredients; pour into pitcher. Garnish each serving with a small chunk or wedge of melon.* See also Watermelon Margarita, *this page.*

RAZZARITA: *Substitute Chambord for the triple sec. Garnish each serving with 3 fresh raspberries speared on a cocktail pick.*

TOP-SHELF MARGARITA: *Use a premium tequila (such as Sauza's Conmemorativo or Cuervo's 1800) and substitute Cointreau for the triple sec.*

WATERMELON MARGARITA *(makes about fifteen 8-ounce servings): Use a pitcher that holds at least 125 ounces and 10-ounce glasses (12-ounce if serving over ice). In a blender, puree in batches 10 heaping cups seedless watermelon chunks (watermelon has a lighter flavor than other melons, so more is needed). Since even seedless watermelon has a few seeds, you may* want to strain the puree before pouring it into the pitcher. Add remaining ingredients except water; stir well. If desired, stir in ⅔ cup (scant 6 ounces) Midori or other melon-flavored liqueur. Cover and refrigerate at least 5 hours. Stir again before serving; garnish each serving with a chunk of watermelon and a lime slice.

 MOCKARITA: *Substitute one 750-ml. bottle (25.4 ounces) dealcoholized white wine for the tequila, and Rose's Non-Alcoholic Triple Sec for the regular triple sec. Increase lime juice to 2 cups (16 ounces); omit water.*

Margarita: Mexico in a glass.

—LUCINDA HUTSON,
AMERICAN AUTHOR, DESIGNER

I love my Martinis so vigorously shaken that they're frosty cold, with minute shards of ice floating on the surface. Which is why if anyone had told me a few months ago that a great Martini could be made sans shaking, I'd have told them they were full of . . . That's why I was blown away when I tested batch Martinis and became an instant fan. There are two tricks to pitcher Martinis: adding water and freezing the mixture. The water's necessary to achieve the same silky texture created by shaking (or stirring) the gin or vodka with ice, which melts slightly and produces the requisite smoothness. Freezing makes the Martinis sensuously satiny and exquisitely cold. If you have room in your freezer, pop the Martini glasses in there an hour or so before serving.

This recipe makes extra-dry Martinis—if you want 'em wetter, add vermouth to taste (my husband, Ron, and I don't even let the vermouth flirt with the gin). My very favorite version is the lemon-infused Zestini (see Variations). Dirty Martini fans will want to try the olive-infused "Olivetti" rendition.

one 750-ml. bottle (25.4 ounces) gin or vodka

¾ cup (6 ounces) water

3 tablespoons plus 1 teaspoon (generous
    1½ ounces) dry vermouth

garnish: 10 olives or lemon twists

Combine all ingredients except garnish in a pitcher that holds at least 40 ounces; stir well. Cover and freeze for at least 4 hours. If your freezer won't accommodate the pitcher, pour mix into two smaller containers—for the best texture, this mixture should be kept in the freezer. Serve in 4- to 5-ounce cocktail glasses; garnish each serving as desired.

variations

DIRTY MARTINI: *Add ⅓ to ½ cup olive brine; garnish each serving with an olive.*

MEZCAL MARTINI: *Substitute mezcal for the gin or vodka and ½ cup (4 ounces) Lillet Blanc for the vermouth. Add the zest (colored portion only) from 1 medium orange to the mixture before freezing. Garnish each serving with an orange twist.*

OLIVETTI: *At least 3 days before serving, combine 30 pitted, brine-packed olives (such as Kalamata, Niçoise, or Picholine) with 2 cups of the gin or vodka. Use the back of a fork to slightly mash the olives—you want the olives to keep their shape while releasing their flavor into the liquor. Cover and refrigerate for*

3 days. Strain liquid into pitcher, add remaining ingredients, and freeze as directed. Cover and refrigerate olives. Garnish each serving with 2 or 3 olives speared on a cocktail pick.

PEPPERTINI: *Substitute a pepper-infused gin or vodka such as Absolut Peppar for the regular gin or vodka; garnish each serving with a small jalapeño pepper, pepper-marinated olive, or jalapeño-stuffed olive.*

RUMTINI: *Substitute light rum for the gin or vodka and fresh lime juice for the vermouth; garnish each serving with a lime wedge.*

TEQUINI: *Substitute tequila for the gin or vodka and fresh lime juice for the vermouth; garnish each serving with a lime twist.*

VIOLETTA: *Reduce water to ⅓ cup (scant 3 ounces), omit vermouth, add ⅔ cup (scant 6 ounces) parfait amour.*

ZESTINI: *Before freezing, add the zest (colored portion only) from 2 large lemons or 2 medium oranges; if desired, stir in ½ to 1 teaspoon Pernod or other anise-flavored liqueur. Garnish each serving with a lemon or orange twist.*

I like a good martini,
One or two at the most.
After one I'm under the table,
After two, I'm under the host.

—DOROTHY PARKER,
AMERICAN WRITER, WIT

S linky, sweet, and seductive, just like its namesake Marilyn. This drink's a creamy green color—for a purple glow and seductive orange-vanilla flavor, try the Monroe Amour variation.

2¼ cups (18 ounces) Midori or other melon-
    flavored liqueur
1½ cups (12 ounces) vodka
¾ cup (6 ounces) light rum
⅓ cup (scant 3 ounces) heavy cream
¼ cup (2 ounces) crème de banana
garnish: ten 1-inch chunks honeydew melon

Combine all ingredients except garnish in a pitcher that holds at least 50 ounces; stir well. Cover and refrigerate at least 4 hours. Serve in 5-ounce cocktail glasses; garnish each serving with a melon chunk hooked over the glass rim.

variations

MONROE À LA CRÈME: *Increase cream to 1 cup (8 ounces).*
MONROE AMOUR: *Substitute parfait amour for the Midori; garnish each serving with half an orange slice or a star fruit slice.*

Chilled glassware gives drinks a cold jump-start, so, if you have room in the fridge, chill glasses for at least 30 minutes before using. Or pop them in the freezer for 10 minutes. **Frosty glasses** are even more fun and great for drinks served up, like a Cosmopolitan, Daiquiri, or Martini. Put glasses in the freezer for at least an hour before you need them. For ultra-frost, dip glasses in cold water, shake off any excess, and then freeze. Needless to say, don't pull these iced glasses out of the freezer until you're ready to fill them. And always hold a frosted cocktail glass by its stem so as not to mar the frosted effect on the bowl.

*D*on't leave out the fresh lime juice—it's
needed to balance the sweetness in this tropical
teaser. For a tangy variation, substitute 2$\frac{1}{4}$ cups each
limeade and pineapple juice for the orange-pineapple
juice.

Makes Twelve 6-ounce servings

4$\frac{1}{2}$ cups (36 ounces) orange-pineapple juice

2$\frac{1}{4}$ cups (18 ounces) gold tequila

$\frac{3}{4}$ cup (6 ounces) Licor 43

$\frac{3}{4}$ cup (6 ounces) blue curaçao

$\frac{3}{8}$ cup (3 ounces) crème de banana

$\frac{1}{4}$ cup (2 ounces) Rose's Lime Juice

2 tablespoons (1 ounce) fresh lime juice

garnish: 12 halved orange slices and
    12 maraschino cherries

Combine all ingredients except garnish in a pitcher that
holds at least 80 ounces; stir well. Can be served immediately or covered and refrigerated until ready to serve. Fill
10-ounce double old-fashioned glasses three-quarters full
with ice cubes. Add drink mixture; garnish each serving with
an orange slice and cherry skewered on a cocktail pick.

They say that you may always know the grave of a Virginian as, from the quantity of julep he has drunk, mint invariably springs up where he has been buried.

—FREDERICK MARRYAT,
BRITISH NAVAL OFFICER, WRITER

*P*art of the ritual of making a Mint Julep is to do so one at a time, so this pitcher version is already side-stepping tradition. And since julep aficionados ardently disagree on whether or not to crush (MUDDLE, page 24) the mint (the muddlers prefer a more assertive mint flavor), I'm striking a balance between the two techniques by taking the least complicated route— letting the mint infuse its flavor into the bourbon overnight. After all, pitcher drinks are all about convenience, right?

Makes ten 3.5-ounce servings

3¾ cups (30 ounces) bourbon

½ cup (4 ounces) water

4 cups loosely packed fresh mint leaves

2 to 4 tablespoons superfine sugar

GARNISH: 30 mint sprigs

Combine first three ingredients in a 1½-quart container; stir well. Cover and refrigerate overnight, or at least 12 hours. Strain the liquid into a pitcher that holds at least 45 ounces, pressing down lightly on the mint to extract all the liquid; discard mint. Add sugar to taste, stirring until dis-

solved. Can be served immediately or covered and refrigerated until ready to serve. To serve, put 3 mint sprigs in each
8- to 10-ounce julep cup or collins glass. Fill to the rim with
crushed ice; add scant ½ cup (3.5 ounces) of the drink mixture and give it a brisk stir. Serve with a straw.

American writer Waverly Root once said, "It is the
destiny of mint to be crushed." That's certainly true
when it comes to drinks like Mint Julep and Mojito.
But the thing you need to know about mint is that
about 20 minutes after it's crushed, chopped, or otherwise abused, its emerald-green color begins to turn
an unappetizing dark brownish-green color (we're
talking *ugly*). The trick when making minted pitcher
drinks in advance is to simply strain off the mint
before serving (*see* the Mojito headnote) and then
garnish with fresh green leaves.

his cooling quaff was born in Cuba almost a hundred years ago and is now popular around the globe. As it says in Mint Condition (page 132), the mint will discolor if it sits longer than 20 minutes. No worries—to make it ahead of time, do this: Just before your guests arrive, strain the mixture, toss out the discolored mint, and add a handful of fresh mint leaves to the pitcher. Lastly, although the Mojito [moh-HEE-toh] can be served sans mixer, it's much more refreshing with the added bubbly.

makes twelve 6-ounce servings

1 bunch fresh mint, washed and blotted dry

³/₄ to 1 cup superfine sugar

1¹/₂ cups (12 ounces) freshly squeezed lime
        juice (reserve 12 lime halves)

one 750-ml. bottle (25.4 ounces) light rum

4¹/₂ cups (36 ounces) cold seltzer water or
        club soda

garnish: 12 mint sprigs

Reserve 12 mint sprigs for garnish; refrigerate in a plastic bag. Stem the remaining mint. No more than 20 minutes

before serving, combine mint leaves and sugar in a pitcher that will hold at least 85 ounces. Use a long-handled wooden muddler or spoon to muddle the mint leaves and sugar together for about 30 seconds. Add 12 squeezed lime halves; muddle a few strokes to release the oils in the lime rind. Stir in lime juice and rum. Can be served immediately or covered and refrigerated until ready to serve. Just before serving, slowly add cold seltzer, tilting the pitcher and pouring onto the pitcher's side to retain as much effervescence as possible. Stir gently to combine. To serve, fill 10-ounce tall glasses three-quarters full with crushed ice. Add a squeezed lime half, a few mint leaves, and then the drink mixture. Garnish each serving with a mint sprig; serve with a straw.

variations

MOJITO ESPECIALE: *Substitute spiced rum for the regular rum.*

MOJITO MEZCALI: *Substitute mezcal for the rum.*

NOJITO: *Omit rum; increase seltzer water or club soda to 7½ cups (60 ounces).*

o keep this drink relatively clear, strain the lemon or lime juice through a paper coffee filter or a cotton cloth. But that's certainly not necessary—it's addictive either way.

one 750-ml. bottle (25.4 ounces) gin

1½ cups (12 ounces) parfait amour

½ cup (4 ounces) fresh lemon or lime juice

Garnish: 12 lemon or lime twists

Combine all ingredients except garnish in a pitcher that holds at least 50 ounces; stir well. Cover and freeze 4 hours. Stir, then pour into 5-ounce cocktail glasses; drop a lemon or lime twist into each serving.

Alcohol is like love. The first kiss is magic,
the second is intimate, the third is routine.
After that you take the girl's clothes off.

—RAYMOND CHANDLER,
AMERICAN AUTHOR

*he name of this drink comes from my adorable
brother-in-law Jim McCurdy, who often uses the phrase
as an e-mail sign-off (in Jim-talk, it means "lots of
kisses"). This drink's like a gussied-up Margarita with a
kiss of mint. For a different yet equally exotic flavor,
substitute Licor 43 for the melon liqueur. Using parfait
amour instead of the melon gives this drink a vanilla-
orange flavor. By the way, for those who aren't bilingual,
muchas (Spanish for "many") is pronounced MOO-chahs.*

Makes Ten 4.5-ounce servings

one 750-ml. bottle (25.4 ounces) silver tequila
¾ cup (6 ounces) Midori or other melon-
 flavored liqueur
¾ cup (6 ounces) white crème de menthe
¾ cup (6 ounces) fresh lime juice
½ cup (4 ounces) water
garnish: 10 mint sprigs

Combine all ingredients except garnish in a pitcher that
holds at least 55 ounces; stir well. Cover and refrigerate at
least 4 hours. Serve in 6-ounce cocktail glasses; garnish
each serving with a mint sprig.

*H*ard as I tried, I couldn't find any information on the Mudslide's origins. Suffice it to say, this drink is wildly popular globally, and each country has its own version. In the United Kingdom, for instance, Mudslides are made with Irish cream liqueur, Kahlúa, chocolate milk, and cream (no vodka)—we're talkin' sweet here, guys! There are loads of variations (the dark rum is outstanding!), a few of which follow. No matter which rendition you choose, adding a little whole milk or half-and-half will dilute the alcohol content, reduce sweetness, and enrich the blend.

Makes twelve 3-ounce servings

1½ cups (12 ounces) Irish cream liqueur

1½ cups (12 ounces) Kahlúa

1½ cups (12 ounces) vodka

Combine all ingredients in a pitcher that holds at least 45 ounces; stir well. Can be served immediately or covered and refrigerated until ready to serve. Fill 6-ounce old-fashioned glasses three-quarters full with ice cubes; add drink mixture.

IRISH MUDSLIDE: *Substitute Irish whiskey for the vodka.*

JAMAICAN MUDSLIDE: *Substitute dark rum or spiced rum for the vodka.*

KENTUCKY MUDSLIDE: *Substitute bourbon for the vodka.*

MALTED MUDSLIDE: *Combine 2 to 4 tablespoons malted milk powder with ¼ cup (2 ounces) cream, blending until the mixture is smooth. Stir into Mudslide mixture.*

MOCHA MUDSLIDE: *Add ½ cup (4 ounces) dark chocolate syrup; mix vigorously until thoroughly incorporated.*

MUDSLIDE SHAKE (MAKES TWELVE 7-OUNCE SERVINGS): *Make a pitcher of Mudslides; refrigerate 4 hours. Slightly soften 3 pints premium-quality coffee, chocolate, or vanilla ice cream. Just before serving, combine in a blender half (2¼ cups) of the Mudslide mixture and 1½ pints softened ice cream; blend on high until smooth. Pour into 8- to 10-ounce cocktail glasses. Repeat with remaining Mudslide mixture and ice cream.*

ROCKY MUDSLIDE SHAKE: *Coarsely crumble 30 Oreo cookies. Make Mudslide Shake, as above. Add half the cookie pieces to each batch, blending only until combined (the cookies should still be in little chunks). Pour into 8- to 10-ounce cocktail glasses. If desired, garnish each serving by sprinkling with 1 heaping teaspoon crushed cookie crumbs.*

I only drink to make other people seem more interesting.

—GEORGE JEAN NATHAN,
AMERICAN CRITIC

*T*wo of these fruity, green potions and you may just take on a neonlike glow. Add an exotic touch by substituting mango or papaya juice for the pineapple juice.

2½ cups (20 ounces) pineapple juice

2 cups (16 ounces) orange juice

1½ cups (12 ounces) gold tequila

¾ cup (6 ounces) blue curaçao

¾ cup (6 ounces) Midori or other melon-
   flavored liqueur

⅓ cup (scant 3 ounces) Demerara (151-proof)
   rum

¼ cup (2 ounces) crème de banana

GARNISH: 10 pineapple chunks and
   10 maraschino cherries

Combine all ingredients except garnish in a pitcher that holds at least 75 ounces; stir well. Can be served immediately or covered and refrigerated until ready to serve. Fill 10-ounce tall glasses two-thirds full with ice cubes. Add drink mixture; garnish each serving with pineapple and

cherry skewered on a cocktail pick. For a tiki touch, add a
paper umbrella to each drink.

Lemon
Logic

When you need both the peel and the juice of a lemon
or other citrus fruit, remove the peel first, then cut the
fruit in half and squeeze out the juice. *See also*
Squeeze Play, page 113.

NOT YO' MOMMA'S LEMONADE

*S*uper-easy and lemony, but this potent potable can pack a wallop. Decrease the alcohol level by adding cold water to taste, or make the following lower-alcohol strawberry version.

makes twelve 6-ounce servings

one 12-ounce can thawed frozen lemonade
     concentrate
one 750-ml. bottle (25.4 ounces) vodka
2 cups (16 ounces) spiced rum
2 cups (16 ounces) water
3/4 cup (6 ounces) limoncello or other lemon-
     flavored liqueur
garnish: 10 lemon slices and mint sprigs

Combine all ingredients except garnish in a pitcher that holds at least 85 ounces; stir well. Can be served immediately or covered and refrigerated until ready to serve. Fill 10-ounce tall glasses or wineglasses two-thirds full with ice cubes. Pour in drink mixture; garnish each serving with a lemon slice and mint sprig skewered on a cocktail pick.

BLOUISIANA LEMONADE: *Substitute blue curaçao for the limoncello and add ½ cup crème de banana.*

KENTUCKY LEMONADE: *Substitute bourbon for the rum.*

LEMONADE SLUSHIE: *Place covered pitcher of lemonade in the freezer overnight. Just before serving, stir vigorously.*

MEXICAN LEMONADE: *Substitute silver tequila for the vodka and triple sec for the limoncello.*

NOT YO' MOMMA'S *PINK* LEMONADE: *Use frozen pink lemonade concentrate; substitute ½ cup Chambord and ¼ cup grenadine syrup for the limoncello. Garnish each serving with 3 raspberries speared on a cocktail pick.*

SOUTHERN COMFORT LEMONADE: *Use one 750-ml. bottle Southern Comfort, reduce vodka to 2 cups, omit spiced rum. Garnish each serving with a thin wedge of peeled peach.*

STRAWBERRY LEMONADE (MAKES ABOUT TWELVE 7.5-OUNCE SERVINGS): *Use a pitcher that holds at least 100 ounces. Thaw a 16-ounce package of frozen whole strawberries. Puree in a blender; strain through a fine sieve. Stir puree into the preceding pink lemonade version. Just before serving, stir vigorously. Garnish each serving with a fresh strawberry.*

WATERMELON LEMONADE (MAKES ABOUT TWELVE 8-OUNCE SERVINGS): *Omit water. In a blender, puree 6 cups chopped seedless watermelon. Strain, if desired; stir into lemonade mixture. Just before serving, stir vigorously. Garnish each serving with a watermelon chunk.*

Always do sober what you said you'd do drunk. That will teach you to keep your mouth shut.

—ERNEST HEMINGWAY,
AMERICAN AUTHOR

*T*his takeoff on the Fuzzy Navel (orange juice and peach schnapps) definitely shifts this drink into the adult category. Use reposado tequila for a more assertive flavor.

2 cups (16 ounces) silver tequila

2 cups (16 ounces) peach schnapps

7 cups (56 ounces) cold fresh orange juice

garnisн: 10 orange slices

Combine all ingredients except garnish in a pitcher that holds at least 100 ounces; stir well. Can be served immediately or covered and refrigerated until ready to serve. Fill 10-ounce cocktail glasses or wineglasses two-thirds full with ice cubes. Add drink mixture; garnish each serving with an orange slice hooked over the glass rim.

variations

FUZZY MELON: *Substitute Midori or other melon-flavored liqueur for the peach schnapps. Garnish each serving with a honeydew melon chunk.*

FUZZLESS NAVEL: *Omit tequila and peach schnapps. Use the following proportions: 2 1/2 cups (20 ounces) peach nectar and 8½ cups (68 ounces) fresh orange juice.*

Turn almost any drink (except those that are high proof and mostly alcohol-based) into a "slushie" by freezing it in the pitcher overnight. Stir just before serving.

*I*t makes perfect sense that the Piña Colada
[PEEN-yah koh-LAH-dah] originated in rum country—
Puerto Rico. The name is Spanish for "strained pineapple," but this popular drink is much more than
that—simply put, it's the taste of the tropics. Don't forget to stir the cream of coconut until smooth before
measuring. For a less sweet drink, reduce the cream of
coconut to 1¼ cups (10 ounces) and increase the
pineapple juice to 4¾ cups (38 ounces). Or leave the
proportions as they are and add ½ cup (4 ounces) fresh
lime juice.

MAKES TEN 7-OUNCE SERVINGS

4 cups (32 ounces) pineapple juice

2 cups (16 ounces) light or gold rum

2 cups (16 ounces) cream of coconut

4 cups crushed ice

GARNISH: 10 half-slices of pineapple and
      10 maraschino cherries

**Combine all ingredients except crushed ice and garnish in a
pitcher that holds at least 100 ounces; stir well. Can be**

served immediately or covered and refrigerated until ready to serve. Just before serving, add crushed ice and stir vigorously. Pour into 8- to 10-ounce tall glasses or wineglasses; garnish each serving with a half-slice of pineapple and a cherry skewered on a cocktail pick.

VARIATIONS

BANANA COLADA: *Reduce pineapple juice to 3½ cups (28 ounces) and cream of coconut to 1½ cups (12 ounces); add 1 cup (8 ounces) crème de banana. Garnish each serving with a banana slice that's been dipped in lime juice.*

BERRY COLADA: *Omit crushed ice. Thaw one 16-ounce package frozen strawberries. Puree in a blender with the cream of coconut. Strain puree, if desired; stir into other ingredients.*

BLUE HAWAIIAN: *Add 1 cup (8 ounces) blue curaçao.*

CHI CHI: *Substitute vodka for the rum.*

MANGO COLADA: *Substitute mango nectar for the pineapple juice. Garnish each serving with a slice of fresh mango.*

MELON COLADA: *Reduce pineapple juice to 3 cups (24 ounces) and add 1 cup (8 ounces) Midori melon liqueur. Garnish each serving with a chunk of honeydew melon.*

PIÑA COLADA FLOAT: *Use 10- to 12-ounce glasses. Place a small scoop of vanilla or coconut ice cream or pineapple sherbet into each glass; top with Piña Colada. Accompany each serving with a spoon and a straw.*

SPICY COLADA: *Substitute spiced rum for the light or gold rum and add ½ cup Goldschläger or other cinnamon schnapps.*

TEQUILADA: *Substitute silver tequila for the rum.*

NADA COLADA: *Omit rum. Increase pineapple juice to 5 cups (40 ounces), cream of coconut to 2½ cups (20 ounces), and crushed ice to 5 cups.*

*W*e have Henry C. Ramos to thank for this creamy concoction. The owner of New Orleans's Imperial Cabinet saloon created this eponymous drink in 1888, and it's been a Big Easy specialty ever since. It's definitely a favorite of mine and makes the perfect potable for a special brunch or lunch.

MAKES TEN 6-OUNCE SERVINGS

one 750-ml. bottle (25.4 ounces) gin

3 cups (24 ounces) heavy cream or half-and-half

3/4 cup (6 ounces) fresh lemon juice

3/4 cup (6 ounces) fresh lime juice

2 tablespoons superfine sugar

Scant 1/2 teaspoon orange flower water

two 10-ounce bottles icy-cold seltzer water or club soda

GARNISH: 10 orange slices

Combine all ingredients except seltzer water and garnish in a pitcher that holds at least 90 ounces; stir vigorously. Cover and refrigerate at least 4 hours. Just before serving, slowly add the seltzer water, tilting the pitcher and pouring onto the pitcher's side to retain as much effervescence as possible. Stir gently to combine. Serve in 10-ounce tall glasses or wineglasses; garnish each serving with an orange slice, hooking it over the glass rim.

What happens when it never comes the way you want it? Like music that never reaches a pitch? What do you do? Go on singing songs and drinking Ramos Fizzes.

—LIZABETH SCOTT,
AMERICAN ACTRESS,
IN THE FILM *DEAD RECKONING*

here are several good raspberry vodkas on the market, including Burnett's Raspberry Vodka, Smirnoff's Raspberry Twist Vodka, and Stolichnaya Raspberry Vodka (Stoli Razberi). Rum lovers may want to substitute Cabana Boy Raspberry Rum for the vodka.

Makes ten 6.5-ounce servings

2¹/₂ cups (20 ounces) raspberry-flavored vodka

2¹/₂ cups (20 ounces) cranberry-raspberry juice

²/₃ cup (scant 6 ounces) Chambord

2¹/₂ cups (20 ounces) icy-cold lime-flavored
    sparkling water

Garnish: 30 fresh raspberries

Combine all ingredients except sparkling water and garnish in a pitcher that holds at least 75 ounces; stir well. Cover and refrigerate at least 4 hours. Just before serving, slowly add sparkling water, tilting the pitcher and pouring onto the pitcher's side to retain as much effervescence as possible. Stir gently to combine. Fill 10-ounce wineglasses three-quarters full with ice cubes. Add drink mixture; garnish each serving with 3 raspberries speared on a cocktail pick.

There's nought, no doubt, so much the spirit calms as rum and true religion.

—LORD BYRON,
BRITISH POET

or a real rush, FLOAT *(page 17) a teaspoon of*
Demerara *(151-proof) rum on top of each serving.*

Makes Ten 6-ounce servings

3 cups (24 ounces) pineapple juice

1½ cups (12 ounces) spiced rum

1 cup (8 ounces) dark rum

¾ cup (6 ounces) Malibu coconut rum

¾ cup (6 ounces) orange curaçao

⅔ cup (scant 6 ounces) grenadine syrup

garnish: 10 half-slices of pineapple

**Combine all ingredients except garnish in a pitcher that
holds at least 70 ounces; stir well. Can be served immediately or covered and refrigerated until ready to serve. Fill
10-ounce tall glasses three-quarters full with crushed ice.
Add drink mixture; garnish each serving with half a pineapple slice.**

*Abstainer, n. A weak person who yields
to the temptation of denying himself
a pleasure.*

—AMBROSE BIERCE,
AMERICAN SATIRIST,
THE DEVIL'S DICTIONARY

*L*ong a party favorite, Sangría [san-GREE-uh] is perfect for pitchers and a sure crowd-pleaser. The variation for Cava Drink (popular in tapas bars) is a Sangría rendition made with cava, a sparkling wine from Spain's Catalan region.

Makes about ten 8-ounce servings

two 750-ml. bottles (50.8 ounces) red wine (Zinfandel, Cabernet Sauvignon, or Burgundy)

3/4 cup (6 ounces) triple sec or other orange-flavored liqueur

3/4 cup (6 ounces) fresh orange juice

1/2 cup (4 ounces) brandy

3/8 cup (3 ounces) fresh lemon or lime juice

1/2 cup (approximately) superfine sugar

2 cups (16 ounces) icy-cold orange-flavored sparkling water

Garnish: 1 orange, 1 lemon, 2 limes, sliced

Combine the first five ingredients in a pitcher that holds at least 100 ounces. Sweeten to taste with sugar, stirring to dissolve. Cover and refrigerate at least 4 hours. Just before serving, slowly add sparkling water, tilting the pitcher and

pouring onto the pitcher's side to retain as much effervescence as possible. Stir gently to combine. Add fruit slices.
Fill 12-ounce wineglasses two-thirds full with ice cubes;
add Sangría and a slice or two of fruit.

CAVA DRINK: *Substitute cold cava for the red wine, increase brandy to ¾ cup (6 ounces), and omit lemon
(or lime) juice and sugar. Have all the ingredients
cold and mix at the last minute. For the fruit, use 1
sliced orange and 1 pint strawberries, hulled and
halved.*

CHAMPAGNE SANGRÍA: *Substitute cold brut or extra-dry
champagne for the red wine. Have all the ingredients
cold and mix at the last minute. In addition to the orange and lemon slices, add about 20 green grapes.*

SANGRÍA BLANCA: *Substitute dry white wine (Chardonnay, Sauvignon Blanc, etc.) for the red wine, and 2
sliced, pitted, peeled peaches for the sliced orange.*

SANGRÍA LIBRE ("FREE"): *Substitute dealcoholized
red wine for the regular wine and Rose's Non-
Alcoholic Triple Sec for the orange-flavored liqueur;
omit brandy.*

SPARKLING SANGRÍA LIBRE: *Substitute dealcoholized sparkling wine for the regular wine and
Rose's Non-Alcoholic Triple Sec for the orange-
flavored liqueur; omit brandy.*

When Coors took its beer slogan "Turn It Loose" south of the border, it was translated as "Suffer from Diarrhea." Needless to say, it was the sales that suffered.

*angrita [san-GREE-tuh], a tomato
juice–orange juice blend with a hot-chile kick, is used
in Mexico as a chaser for tequila shots. Why not,
I thought, combine the Sangrita with the tequila and
sip it rather than shoot it? The result is Sangrita
Simpático, an exotic-tasting blend that earns raves at
brunches. Any hot pepper sauce can be used—one of my
favorites is Cholula, a Mexican sauce based on the
fiery pequín chiles. Green Tabasco (jalapeño-based) is
also very good. This drink is supposed to be spicy, but
it's best to start slowly—you can always add more hot
sauce after you taste.*

Makes ten 5.5-ounce servings

2¼ cups (18 ounces) silver or gold tequila

1½ cups (12 ounces) tomato juice

1½ cups (12 ounces) fresh orange juice

¾ cup (6 ounces) fresh lime juice

¾ cup (6 ounces) grenadine syrup

2 teaspoons Worcestershire sauce

1 to 1½ teaspoons hot pepper sauce

1 teaspoon salt

½ teaspoon ground allspice

ɢᴀʀɴɪꜱʜ: 12 orange slices

If desired, moisten the rims of ten 8-ounce wineglasses with a little orange juice, then dip rim into salt (for other options, see DECORATED GLASS RIMS, page 47). Put glasses in the fridge if you have room. Combine all ingredients except garnish in a pitcher that holds at least 65 ounces; stir well. Cover and refrigerate at least 4 hours. Fill prepared glasses three-quarters full with crushed ice. Add drink mixture; garnish each serving with an orange slice, hooking it over the rim. Serve with a straw.

variations

SPARKLING SANGRITA SIMPÁTICO *(makes ten 7.5-ounce servings): Use a pitcher that holds at least 90 ounces. Make the Sangrita Simpático recipe as usual. Just before serving, slowly add 2½ cups (20 ounces) icy-cold orange- or lime-flavored sparkling water, tilting the pitcher and pouring onto the pitcher's side to retain as much effervescence as possible. Stir gently to combine. Serve in 10-ounce wineglasses filled two-thirds full with ice cubes.*

 SANGRITA NEATA: *Omit the tequila. Use the following proportions: 2 cups (16 ounces) tomato juice, 2 cups (16 ounces) fresh orange juice, 1 cup (8 ounces) fresh lime juice, and 1 cup (8 ounces) grenadine syrup. Add ¾ cup (6 ounces) water.*

*Even though a number of people have
tried, no one has yet found a way to drink
for a living.*

—JEAN KERR,
AMERICAN AUTHOR,
PLAYWRIGHT

I shared my first Scorpion years ago (I'm not telling!) with a delicious guy named Ron. We were at Trader Vic's in Beverly Hills, where the lighting was dim and the mood seductive as we shared a Scorpion Bowl for four. And then we ordered another. It was love at first sip of the Scorpion . . . and Ron's now my husband. The classic Tahitian garnish for a Scorpion is a gardenia, but orange slices will do in a pinch.

Makes ten 8-ounce servings

2½ cups (20 ounces) light or gold rum

2½ cups (20 ounces) fresh orange juice

1¾ cups (14 ounces) fresh lemon juice

1¼ cups (10 ounces) brandy

⅔ cup (scant 6 ounces) orgeat syrup

4 cups crushed ice

garnish: 10 pesticide-free gardenias or
     10 orange slices

Combine all ingredients except crushed ice and garnish in a pitcher that holds at least 100 ounces; stir well. Can be served immediately or covered and refrigerated until ready to serve. Just before serving, add crushed ice and stir vigorously. Fill 12-ounce tall glasses two-thirds full with ice cubes. Add drink mixture; garnish each serving with a gardenia or an orange slice and serve with straws.

Anagrammatically Yours

Here's one for you: The word "excitation" is an anagram for "intoxicate." Even better—the cognate anagram (one in which the letters form another word or phrase that either redefines or is close to the original meaning) for "distillation" is "do it in a still"! Which brings to mind what American novelist William Faulkner once said: "Civilization begins with distillation."

*S*cotch has long been married with liqueurs in cocktails, but this simple yet sophisticated cocktail takes an exotic twist with the flavor of ginger.

makes ten 3.5-ounce servings

> 2½ cups (20 ounces) blended Scotch
> 1¼ cups (10 ounces) Canton Delicate Ginger
>   Liqueur
> ⅔ cup (scant 6 ounces) Cointreau
> 2½ teaspoons Galliano
> garnish: ten ¼-by-2-inch strips of candied
>   ginger plus 10 orange twists

Combine all ingredients except garnish in a pitcher that holds at least 45 ounces; stir well. Cover and refrigerate at least 4 hours. Pour into 5-ounce cocktail glasses; garnish each serving by dropping in a ginger strip and orange twist.

his drink has multiple versions and forms—the original was served as a shooter. Whether you use orange, pineapple, or grapefruit juice is purely personal preference. If you like a tarter drink, go for the grapefruit juice—pineapple juice produces the sweetest version.

MAKES TEN 8-OUNCE SERVINGS

3³/₄ cups (30 ounces) cranberry juice

3³/₄ cups (30 ounces) fresh orange juice or
  unsweetened grapefruit juice or pineapple
  juice

1¹/₄ cups (10 ounces) vodka

1¹/₄ cups (10 ounces) peach schnapps

GARNISH: 10 maraschino cherries with stems

Combine all ingredients except garnish in a pitcher that holds at least 90 ounces; stir well. Can be served immediately or covered and refrigerated until ready to serve. Fill 12-ounce tall glasses two-thirds full with ice cubes. Add drink mixture; garnish each serving with a cherry.

SAFE SEX ON THE BEACH: *Omit vodka and schnapps; add 2 cups (16 ounces) peach nectar and ½ cup water.*

An alcoholic is someone you don't like who drinks as much as you do.

—DYLAN THOMAS,
WELSH POET

*S*hrubs, which originated in England cen-
turies ago, were initially simply macerations of fruit
and liquor. Nonalcoholic versions were a combo of
fruit, vinegar, and sugar. This modern-day rendition
combines the best of both worlds, delivering a potion
that's both sassy and refreshing. Dark rum is the key
here—light rum just won't produce the body this drink
needs. And although I prefer seltzer water for its clean
flavor, soda water may be substituted in a pinch.

maKes twelve 7.5-ounce servings

1⅛ cups (9 ounces) good-quality raspberry
    vinegar
1⅛ cups granulated sugar
one 750-ml. bottle (25.4 ounces) dark rum
¾ cup (6 ounces) spiced rum
6 cups (48 ounces) icy-cold seltzer water
garnish: 12 mint sprigs

**Combine the first four ingredients in a pitcher that holds at
least 100 ounces; stir well. Can be served immediately or
covered and refrigerated until ready to serve. Just before
serving, slowly add seltzer water, tilting the pitcher and**

pouring onto the pitcher's side to retain as much effervescence as possible. Stir gently to combine. Fill 12-ounce tall glasses or wineglasses two-thirds full with ice cubes. Add drink mixture; garnish each serving with a mint sprig.

Twas a woman who drove me to drink, and I never had the courtesy to thank her for it.

—W. C. FIELDS,
AMERICAN COMEDIAN, ACTOR

For a different take on this refreshing sipper, try a combination of cranberry-raspberry juice and pineapple-orange juice.

MAKES TEN 6.5-OUNCE SERVINGS

3 cups (24 ounces) cranberry juice

2 cups (16 ounces) fresh orange juice

2 cups (16 ounces) dark rum

1 cup (8 ounces) spiced rum

$1/3$ cup (scant 3 ounces) grenadine syrup

GARNISH: 10 orange slices

Combine all ingredients except garnish in a pitcher that holds at least 75 ounces; stir well. Can be served immediately or covered and refrigerated until ready to serve. Fill 10-ounce cocktail, tall, or double old-fashioned glasses two-thirds full with ice cubes. Add drink mixture; garnish each serving with an orange slice hooked over the glass rim.

VARIATION

BOURBON HOUSE SLIDER: *Substitute bourbon for the dark rum and Southern Comfort for the spiced rum.*

Work is the curse of the drinking classes.

—MIKE ROMANOFF,
AMERICAN RESTAURATEUR

a kick-back-and-relax summer refresher that's equally wonderful when limeade is substituted for the pineapple juice. For an even more tropical flavor, use spiced rum for half the dark rum and crème de banana for the Licor 43.

makes ten 7.5-ounce servings

4 cups (32 ounces) pineapple juice

2½ cups (20 ounces) dark rum

1 cup (8 ounces) fresh lime juice

⅔ cup (scant 6 ounces) Licor 43

⅔ cup (scant 6 ounces) grenadine syrup

½ cup (4 ounces) water

3 tablespoons (1½ ounces) thawed frozen
   orange juice concentrate

garnish: 10 pineapple wedges and 10 orange
   slices

Combine all ingredients except garnish in a pitcher that holds at least 85 ounces; stir well. Can be served immediately or covered and refrigerated until ready to serve. Fill 12-ounce tall glasses two-thirds full with ice cubes. Add drink mixture; garnish each serving with a pineapple wedge and orange slice skewered on a cocktail pick.

*T*his oh-so-smooth, low-alcohol sipper is perfect for the long, hot days of summer. For a completely different, but equally wonderful, flavor, try substituting peach schnapps for the melon liqueur.

5 cups (40 ounces) Southern Comfort

2 cups (16 ounces) fresh orange juice

1 cup (8 ounces) Midori or other melon-
    flavored liqueur

3/4 cup (6 ounces) fresh lemon juice

garnish: 12 half-slices of orange and
    12 maraschino cherries

Combine all ingredients except garnish in a pitcher that holds at least 80 ounces; stir well. Can be served immediately or covered and refrigerated until ready to serve. Fill 10-ounce wineglasses three-quarters full with crushed ice; add drink mixture. Garnish each serving with orange slice and cherry skewered on a cocktail pick; serve with a straw.

Whenever I'm caught between two evils,
I take the one I've never tried.

—MAE WEST,
AMERICAN ACTRESS

*T*his capricious quencher marries the tart sweetness of lemonade with the slightly bitter Pimm's—the
rum adds a spicy finish. The result is a smooth mouthful
that makes you want it to last and last and last. Word
to the wise: Too many of these sneaky sippers and the
next morning'll feel like a summer bummer.

makes ten 6.5-ounce servings

¾ cup (6 ounces) thawed frozen lemonade
   concentrate
one 750-ml. bottle (25.4 ounces) Pimm's No. 1
3 cups (24 ounces) cold water
1½ cups (12 ounces) spiced rum
garnish: 10 lemon slices

Combine all ingredients except garnish in a pitcher that
holds at least 75 ounces; stir well. Can be served immediately or covered and refrigerated until ready to serve. Fill
10-ounce wineglasses or tall glasses three-quarters full
with ice cubes. Add drink mixture; garnish each serving with
a lemon slice hooked over the glass rim.

DEMINTED SUMMER HUMMER: *Combine 2 cups washed mint leaves with lemonade concentrate;* MUDDLE *(page 24) for 30 seconds. Add remaining ingredients, stirring well. Cover and refrigerate for at least 2 hours. Strain liquid; discard mint. Just before serving, pour drink mixture back into pitcher and add 1 cup washed mint leaves; garnish each serving with a mint sprig.*

SPARKLING SUMMER HUMMER: *Omit water. Combine remaining liquid ingredients in pitcher and refrigerate. Just before serving, slowly add 3 cups (24 ounces) icy-cold seltzer water or club soda, tilting the pitcher and pouring onto the pitcher's side to retain as much effervescence as possible. Stir gently to combine.*

*T*hough there are several tales of this drink's origin, the most popular is that it was created at Hollywood's Don the Beachcomber restaurant in the thirties. Wherever and whenever it began, this one's serious and, unless no one's driving, should be limited to one per person. Whatever you do, have plenty of munchies to balance the booze. The Demerara rum can either be mixed in with the rest of the ingredients or floated on the surface, as is traditional.

Makes ten 8-ounce servings

2½ cups (20 ounces) light rum

1¼ cups (10 ounces) dark rum

1¼ cups (10 ounces) passion fruit syrup

1¼ cups (10 ounces) pineapple juice

1¼ cups (10 ounces) fresh orange juice

1¼ cups (10 ounces) fresh lime juice

⅔ cup (scant 6 ounces) apricot brandy

⅓ cup (scant 3 ounces) grenadine syrup

⅜ cup (3 ounces) Demerara (151-proof) rum

garnish: 10 *each* pineapple spears, orange
    slices, maraschino cherries, and mint sprigs

Combine all ingredients except Demerara rum (unless you're going to mix it in) and garnish in a pitcher that holds at least 90 ounces; stir well. Can be served immediately or covered and refrigerated until ready to serve. Fill 12-ounce tall or hurricane glasses three-quarters full with ice cubes. Add drink mixture. If you haven't added the Demerara rum to the drink already, FLOAT (page 17) 2 teaspoons of it on the surface of each drink; don't mix. Garnish each serving with a pineapple spear, orange slice, cherry, and mint sprig.

variation

ZOMBARILLA: *Omit apricot brandy, reduce grenadine syrup to ¼ cup (2 ounces), and add ¾ cup (6 ounces) crème de banana. Garnish each serving with a banana slice.*

It is, of course, true that we can be intemperate in eating as well as in drinking, but the results of the intemperance would appear to be different. After a fifth helping of rice pudding one does not become overfamiliar with strangers, nor does an extra slice of ham inspire a man to beat his wife.

—A. A. MILNE,
ENGLISH AUTHOR, DRAMATIST

At every party there are two kinds of people—
those who want to go home and those
who don't. The trouble is, they are usually
married to each other.

—ANN LANDERS,
AMERICAN ADVICE COLUMNIST,
AUTHOR

Party Food Ideas for People Who Don't Like to Cook

LET'S FACE IT—POTATO CHIPS AND DIPS ARE PASS-able party fare but, with a little thought, you can do so-o-o-o much better with relatively little ef-fort. Following are dozens of ideas for quick munchies to go with pitcher drinks. Many of these tidbits can be found ready-to-go in delis and markets, others in the supermarket frozen-food section, and still others you can throw together in minutes. And it only takes a little more effort to dress up store-bought party food by adding a few simple garnishes like CELERY and SCALLION BRUSHES (page 44), CHILE PEPPER FLOWERS (page 45), or

CARROT CURLS (page 44). So here are some party-food ideas to give your imagination a jump-start for creative, easy alternatives to chips and dip.

BAGEL CHIPS *A nice change of pace from chips, these crunchy dipsters are available in most supermarkets. Or you can make your own:* Cut bagels crosswise into ⅛-inch slices and arrange in a single layer on a greased baking sheet. If desired, lightly brush the slices with extra-virgin olive oil and sprinkle with salt, herbs, sesame seeds, or other toppings. Bake in a preheated 350°F oven for 5 minutes a side, or until crisp and golden brown.

BREADSTICKS For portable cocktail food, it's hard to beat breadsticks. They come soft, crisp, and in myriad shapes and flavors. Serve by standing them upright in a glass, pitcher, brandy snifter, and so on.

Wrapped breadsticks: For a super-easy cocktail nibble, wrap breadsticks around the middle with thin slices of prosciutto, smoked salmon, or cheese (the latter should be at room temperature so it's pliable). Place the "wrap" material on a flat surface, position the breadstick along one edge, and roll it up so that the wrap is around the breadstick's middle. Arrange on a plate and watch 'em go.

BRIE IN PUFF PASTRY You'll find this in the cheese section of many markets. Just bake according to directions and serve warm with French baguette slices or CROSTINI (page 185).

BRIE with CHUTNEY Set a 2-pound wheel of Brie (rind intact) on a serving plate; cover and bring to room temperature. Just before serving, spoon about 1$\frac{1}{2}$ cups of room-temperature or slightly warm mango, tomato, or cranberry chutney (cutting up any large pieces of fruit) over the Brie's surface. Gild the lily by sprinkling with 1 cup toasted walnuts.

CAVIAR It should be a given that you buy only fresh (not pasteurized) caviar and the best you can afford. Beluga, osetra, and sevruga, in that order, are considered by many to be the finest, although the rich orange-colored salmon "caviar" is also excellent. Buy caviar at the last minute and keep it in the coldest part of the refrigerator. Take it out of the fridge 30 minutes before serving; open just before serving. Use wood, glass, or mother-of-pearl serving spoons—metal causes caviar to oxidize and change color. The finer the caviar, the less embellishment it needs. Serve it in a bowl over ice, accompanied by store-bought buckwheat blini (mini Russian pancakes, the traditional vehicle for caviar), toast points, or CROSTINI (page 185), and tiny lemon wedges for spritzing. If you like, accompany the caviar with store-bought crème fraîche or sour cream. Reserve trappings like chopped onion and hard-cooked eggs for less expensive caviars.

CHEESE See BRIE IN PUFF PASTRY (page 182), BRIE WITH CHUTNEY (page 183), CHEESE STICKS (below), CHEESE TRAY (below), CHILI CON QUESO (page 185), FRICO (page 189), and MARINATED BOCCONCINI (page 192).

CHEESE STICKS You'll find these crispy pastries in gourmet markets, delis, and some supermarkets. They come in various flavors including Cheddar, Parmesan, peppered, and herbed. Serve by standing them up in a tall wineglass or small pitcher.

CHEESE TRAY A selection of cheeses is probably one of the least labor-intensive party nibbles to create. Three or four types of cheese are sufficient—choose an assortment with varying shapes, textures, and colors. For example, a goat's-milk cheese (banon, Bucheron, Montrachet), a blue cheese (Gorgonzola, Maytag Blue, Stilton), a firm or semifirm cheese (Asiago, Cheddar, dry Jack, Parmesan), and a soft cheese (Brie, Camembert, Epoisses de Bourgogne, Explorateur). Set out a large basket of fresh or toasted baguette slices or crackers.

If a cheese tray is your primary party nibble, accompany it with companions such as olives (if the olives have pits, set out a small bowl for discards), toasted or seasoned nuts, or ROASTED GARLIC (page 196). Fruit is a natural pairing for cheese—apples, pears, and grapes all work well. Be sure to take the cheese tray out of the refrigerator 30 to 45 minutes before guests arrive to allow the cheese to reach room temperature, where it will have maximum flavor.

CHILI CON QUESO *There's no room in my recipe repertoire for processed cheese . . . except for this dip, which just isn't as gooey without it.* In a medium, heavy saucepan, combine 1 pound pasteurized processed cheese (cut into large chunks); one 7-ounce can mild tomato-based salsa; 2 to 4 tablespoons minced jalapeños (they come canned) or chipotle peppers; 2 garlic cloves, minced (or $1/4$ teaspoon garlic powder); and 2 teaspoons chili powder. Cook over low heat, stirring frequently, until cheese is melted and mixture is homogenous, about 8 minutes. Serve warm with tortilla chips. Makes about 3 cups.

CHINESE TAKE-OUT Bite-size dim sum, such as pot stickers, fried won tons, shu mai, and har gao, are all easy finger food. Or you can buy the same thing frozen and heat in the oven at the last minute.

CROSTINI *Many stores sell bags or boxes of crostini (toasted bread rounds), plain and flavored. To make your own:* Cut French baguettes into $1/4$-inch-thick slices. Lightly brush one side with extra-virgin olive oil (seasoned or plain). Bake in a preheated 400°F oven for about 10 minutes, or until crisp and golden.

CRUDITÉS WITH DIP Serving crudités (fresh veggies) is easier today because so many markets carry vegetables already cleaned and cut. But a crudités platter is pretty easy anyway, and certainly requires no cooking. Here are some suggestions for vegetables you can use to create a colorful arrangement: sugar snap or snow peas, cauliflower and broccoli florets, strips of green, yellow, and red bell pepper, cherry tomatoes in a variety of colors, radishes, slices of peeled turnip or celery root, chunks of jicama, endive leaves, sliced fennel, cucumber and zucchini slices or sticks, crisp-cooked asparagus spears or green beans, and so on. Any dip will do (*see* DIPPITY DOO DAH, page 187), although you'll want something with body so it will cling to the vegetables.

CURRIED PUMPKIN-SEED DIP *A perfect dip for shrimp, crudités, ham chunks, crackers, pita crisps, whatever.* In a medium bowl, combine ¾ cup plain, low-fat yogurt; ¾ cup mayonnaise; 1 cup ground, toasted, hulled pumpkin seeds; 2 tablespoons minced scallions; 1 tablespoon lemon juice; 1 teaspoon curry powder; and ¼ teaspoon garlic powder. Cover and refrigerate for at least 2 hours. Remove from refrigerator 30 minutes before serving. Makes about 2½ cups.

DIPPITY DOO DAH *No doubt about it, dips are one of the most popular party foods and there are myriad store-bought styles available, including spinach, artichoke, roasted eggplant, hummus, cheese, French onion, crab, and salmon. It just doesn't get any easier. However, the sad truth is that some dips have that strange store-bought flavor (blame it on the additives). No worries, mate—here's how you can jazz up and disguise them:* For each cup of dip, stir in 1 tablespoon each good-quality olive oil, freshly squeezed lemon or lime juice, and minced fresh herbs (parsley, basil, cilantro, tarragon, dill, etc.). Other additions could include $1/4$ to $1/2$ teaspoon freshly ground pepper, cayenne, curry powder, chili powder, or powdered ginger. Or a tablespoon or two of grated Parmesan or Asiago, or finely chopped sun-dried tomatoes, roasted red peppers, pitted olives, or toasted nuts. Personalizing store-bought dips makes them "yours" and you don't need to tell anyone otherwise. *See also* CHILI CON QUESO (page 185), CURRIED PUMPKIN-SEED DIP (page 186), GINGER-PEANUT DIP (page 191), and GUACAMOLE (page 191).

Dip Containers: Serving dips in bowls (plastic's tacky) is the usual way to go, but edible containers add pizzazz to the presentation. Consider large bell peppers (red, yellow, orange, green), eggplants, oversize tomatoes, or red or green cabbages. Halve and hollow out such vegetables and you have a "bowl" for the dip.

DIPSTERS No doubt about it, dips are back, but there's no need to settle on serving them with the ubiquitous potato chips. There are myriad other dipsters, including BAGEL CHIPS (page 182) and PITA CHIPS (page 195), both of which are available commercially packaged. Or use scissors to quickly cut thin, store-bought focaccia into irregular chunks. Or serve dips with CRUDITÉS (page 186), crunchy BREADSTICKS (page 182), pretzels, or a selection of small and unusually shaped crackers. Of course, if you want to serve chips with your dip, they don't have to be *ordinary*. There are loads of interesting options—blue (and red) corn chips, TERRA CHIPS (page 198), and popped corn chips, just to name a few.

EDAMAME AND/OR SUGAR SNAP PEAS Cooked edamame (Japanese soybeans) are available in Asian markets as well as the produce sections of many supermarkets. Serve them as is, in their furry little pods, letting guests snap them open and pop out the peas. Have a bowl on hand for pod discards. The sugar snaps are completely edible. If you like, set out a bowl of mixed salt and cracked pepper, for those who wish to dip.

FAUX FOCACCIA *This one couldn't be easier and will have guests asking for more.* Unroll a 10-ounce tube of Pillsbury Pizza Crust and place it on a greased baking sheet. It'll measure about 8½ by 10 inches—don't stretch it. Lightly brush dough with extra-virgin olive oil; sprinkle with salt, pepper, and 1 to 2 tablespoons finely chopped fresh herbs (basil, tarragon, oregano) or 2 teaspoons fennel seeds (or both). Use the back of a spoon to lightly press herbs or seeds into dough. Sprinkle with 3 tablespoons grated Asiago or Parmesan cheese. Bake in a preheated 400°F oven for 10 to 13 minutes, or until golden brown. Immediately cut 6 strips lengthwise and 3 crosswise (I use kitchen shears); serve warm. Makes 18 strips.

FREEZER FINDS There's bound to be an appetizer or two in your supermarket's freezer section that will please your guests. Among the choices I found recently are: cheese-stuffed jalapeños (also called poppers), buffalo wings, dim sum, pot stickers, egg rolls, meatballs, cheese-topped bagel bites, pigs in blankets, breaded mozzarella sticks, mini crab cakes, mini quiches, pizzas, savory turnovers, cheese-and-bacon-topped potato skins, and popcorn shrimp. Any of these can be popped into the oven just as guests begin arriving and served hot in minutes.

FRICO *No one will believe how easy these thin, crispy cheese wafers are, so don't tell. Montasio cheese is traditional in Italy, but frico [FREE-koh] can be made with other cheeses, including Parmesan, Asiago, Cheddar, and Gruyère. For each cup of grated cheese (which yields about 12 wafers),* add 1 tablespoon flour. You can also add $\frac{1}{4}$ teaspoon cracked black pepper and $1\frac{1}{2}$ teaspoons fresh herbs (or $\frac{1}{2}$ teaspoon dried) per cup of cheese. Toss such additions with the cheese to mix thoroughly. Spray large baking sheets with cooking spray. Place tablespoons of grated cheese about 3 inches apart on baking sheets (stir mixture often to keep smaller ingredients from falling to the bottom of the bowl). Bake in a preheated 375°F oven about 10 minutes, or until golden. Let stand at room temperature a minute or two to firm. Use a metal spatula to transfer to paper towels to blot and cool. May be made several days in advance and stored in an airtight container. Frico are very delicate, so store them in flat layers separated by waxed paper.

GARLICKY HERBED OLIVES *These are best served at room temperature or slightly warm. After the olives are gone, there's a bonus: the oil makes great garlic bread.* In a large, flat-bottomed glass or ceramic bowl, combine 1 cup extra-virgin olive oil, $\frac{1}{4}$ cup lemon juice, the zest of 1 lemon cut into wide strips, 1 tablespoon dried tarragon, 2 teaspoons dried oregano leaves, and 1 teaspoon each dried thyme leaves, salt, and cracked black pepper; stir well. Add 10 garlic cloves (minced) and 1 heaping cup each Kalamata, Niçoise, and Spanish or California green olives. Cover with plastic wrap and microwave on high for 5 minutes, stirring halfway through. Cover and refrigerate 2 days, or at least overnight. Before serving, let stand at room temperature for 30 minutes to take the chill off. Makes about 3½ cups. *See also* OLIVADA (page 193) and OLIVE ASSORTMENT (page 194).

GINGER–PEANUT DIP *Great with chunks of smoked chicken, crudités, and shrimp.* In a blender, combine ¾ cup very hot chicken broth, 1 cup creamy peanut butter, 3 tablespoons low-sodium soy sauce, 3 tablespoons fresh lime juice, 2 peeled garlic cloves, 1 tablespoon minced fresh ginger (or 2 teaspoons powdered ginger), and ¼ to ½ teaspoon cayenne pepper. Cover blender and process until mixture is smooth. Start at low speed and gradually increase to high so hot liquid doesn't burst through lid. If necessary, thin with a little water. Makes about 2 cups.

GREEK PIZZA Split pitas horizontally, sprinkle the inside of each half with cheese (half and half grated mozzarella and crumbled feta), capers, sliced olives, and crumbled oregano. Place on greased baking sheets; broil 6 inches from heat for about 2 minutes, or just until cheese melts. Cut into wedges while warm.

GUACAMOLE *This one's a winner—a simple, four-ingredient guacamole like they serve in Mexico.* Halve and pit 4 ripe Hass avocados; scoop flesh into a medium bowl, discarding peel. Mince 2 medium jalapeño peppers with seeds (wear latex gloves to protect your hands from the chile's volatile oils). You can use 3 to 4 tablespoons minced canned jalapeños, but the flavor won't be as fresh. Add jalapeños and 1 tablespoon fresh lime juice to the avocado in the bowl. Mash ingredients together with a fork, leaving it a little chunky. Salt to taste. Makes about 2 cups.

Guacamole additions: To extend this Mexican-style dip, add any or several of the following: 1 medium finely chopped, seeded tomato; 1 teaspoon chili powder; 2 thinly sliced scallions; 1 tablespoon minced cilantro; or 1 large garlic clove, minced.

HOT-SHOT POPCORN Buy a 6- to 8-ounce bag of salted popped corn; put it in a huge bowl. In a small bowl, combine 2 teaspoons chili powder, $\frac{1}{2}$ teaspoon dried oregano leaves, $\frac{1}{4}$ to $\frac{1}{2}$ teaspoon cayenne, and $\frac{1}{4}$ teaspoon garlic powder. Slowly stir in $\frac{1}{2}$ cup vegetable oil or melted butter. Drizzle half the mixture over the popcorn; toss to coat (your hands will work best). Add remaining oil and toss again. Set out in several small bowls.

MARINATED BOCCONCINI [bohk-kohn-CHEE-nee] *Bocconcini are small, 1-inch nuggets of fresh mozzarella—they have a soft texture and slightly sweet, bland flavor. You'll find them packed in water or whey (usually in plastic tubs) in Italian markets, cheese stores, and many su-*

permarkets. Thoroughly drain two 8-ounce tubs of bocconcini; blot cheese dry with paper towel. In a large bowl, combine $\frac{1}{2}$ cup extra-virgin olive oil, $\frac{1}{4}$ cup minced fresh herbs (a combination of basil, parsley, and mint is nice), 2 medium garlic cloves (minced), and $\frac{1}{2}$ teaspoon each salt and cracked black pepper. Add bocconcini, tossing gently to thoroughly coat with seasoned oil. Cover and refrigerate at least 12 hours and for up to 5 days. Let stand at room temperature for 30 minutes to take the chill off. To serve, mound bocconcini in the center of a platter, surrounded by cherry tomatoes and olives. Accompany with picks for spearing.

NAUGHTY NUTS *These sweet, hot, and sassy nuts are easy and delicious.* In a small bowl, combine 2 tablespoons packed brown sugar, 1 tablespoon Chinese five-spice powder, 2 teaspoons salt, 1 teaspoon ground ginger, and $\frac{1}{2}$ to 1 teaspoon cayenne. Slowly stir in $\frac{1}{3}$ cup vegetable oil or melted unsalted butter. Toss with 4 cups mixed unsalted nuts. Spread nuts in a single layer on 2 rimmed, ungreased baking sheets. Bake in a preheated 325°F oven for 15 minutes. Cool slightly before serving. Store in an airtight container at room temperature for up to 1 week.

OLIVADA *A quick and easy spread that'll garner raves.* Toss 1 large peeled garlic clove into a running food processor fitted with a metal blade; process until bits of garlic are clinging to the sides of the bowl. Scrape down the sides of the bowl and add 3 cups pitted Kalamata or other good-quality black olives, ⅓ cup olive oil, and ½ teaspoon *each* dried oregano, basil, and thyme. Process until mixture is pureed, scraping down sides of bowl as necessary. Cover and refrigerate for up to 2 weeks. Let stand at room temperature for 30 minutes before serving as a spread for crackers, bread rounds, or CROSTINI (page 185). *See also* GARLICKY HERBED OLIVES (page 190) and OLIVE ASSORTMENT (page 194).

OLIVE ASSORTMENT Heap a bowl with a mixture of olives—Kalamata, Niçoise, Spanish, Picholine, Provençal, or stuffed (with anything from pimientos, to almonds, to pickled garlic, to baby onions, to jalapeños). Or serve the olives in large Martini glasses. Here's a trick: Put the olives in a single layer and microwave them on high for a minute or so—the flavor is fantastic. Serve warm olives with picks. *See also* GARLICKY HERBED OLIVES (page 190) and OLIVADA (page 193).

OYSTERS ON THE HALF SHELL Serve on a bed of crushed ice, accompanied with lemon wedges and hot sauce. *See also* SMOKED OYSTERS (page 196).

PÂTÉ SELECTION Excellent freshly made pâtés are available in delis, take-out stores, and charcuteries. There are two basic styles—country pâté (coarse-textured, with chunks of meat) or the smooth, creamy type. Arrange a pâté platter with one or two of each of the styles, accompanied by cornichons (tiny, crisp gherkins available in jars), a good mustard or two, and slices of French baguette.

PITA CHIPS *You can find pita chips at some markets, but it's easy to make your own.* Split pita rounds horizontally and lightly brush the insides with olive oil; salt and pepper to taste. Stack the rounds, then cut the stack into 12 wedges. Arrange wedges closely in a single layer on a lightly oiled baking sheet. Bake in a preheated 350°F oven for 8 to 10 minutes, or until golden brown. Cool to room temperature; store airtight for up to 5 days.

QUICKIE QUESADILLAS *Quesadillas are typically fried, which is messy and time-consuming. Here's the easy way out:* Place 4 large tortillas flat on a working surface. Sprinkle half of each one with ⅓ cup grated cheese (Cheddar, Jack, or a mixture), 1 tablespoon minced jalapeños, and a dusting of chili powder. (If you want to pump it up, add crumbled, crisply cooked bacon or chorizo sausage and chopped cilantro.) Fold uncovered half over filling, forming a half-moon. Place quesadillas on a greased baking sheet; spray the tops with cooking spray. Bake in a preheated 400°F oven for

8 minutes; flip and bake quesadillas an additional 5 minutes, or until golden. Cut each one into 8 wedges. Serve warm. Makes 32 pieces.

ROASTED GARLIC *When garlic is roasted, it turns golden and buttery-soft, its flavor slightly sweet and nutty—perfect for spreading on bread.* Gently rub off the outer layers of papery skin of 2 whole heads of garlic. Separate into cloves and place on a square of aluminum foil large enough to loosely enclose the garlic. Drizzle cloves with about 2 teaspoons olive oil; loosely wrap and seal. Bake in a preheated 400°F oven about 30 minutes, or until soft when pierced with a metal skewer or a knife point. Open foil during final 5 minutes of cooking time. Serve warm or at room temperature, accompanied by plain or toasted baguette slices (*see* CROSTINI, page 185). Refrigerate leftover garlic in an airtight jar for up to 10 days.

SHRIMP PLATTER Purchase cooked, large, tail-on shrimp, arrange in a shallow bowl filled with crushed ice. Accompany with a couple of small bowls of sauce, either store-bought—such as cocktail sauce or homemade—like CURRIED PUMPKIN-SEED DIP (page 186) or GINGER-PEANUT DIP (page 191).

SMOKED OYSTERS These tiny tenders typically come in tins of 3.75 ounces and 8 ounces. Simply drain, blot dry with paper towels, and serve in a bowl with picks for spearing. Accompany with crackers or toast rounds.

SMOKED SALMON TARTARE *This one's particularly great for Martini parties.* In a large bowl, mix 1 pound finely chopped smoked salmon; 2 tablespoons *each* vodka, fresh lime juice, capers, and minced shallots; and 1 tablespoon finely chopped fresh dill (or 1 teaspoon dried dillweed). Salt and pepper to taste. Serve accompanied by French baguette slices or CROSTINI (page 185). Or use the tartare to stuff cherry tomatoes.

SOUSED SAUSAGES In a large bowl (for the microwave) or a large skillet (for the stovetop), combine 1 cup hickory- or mesquite-flavored barbecue sauce, ³⁄₄ cup dark rum or Jack Daniel's whiskey, ½ cup packed dark brown sugar, ½ teaspoon cayenne, and ¼ teaspoon ground cloves. Cut 2 pounds fully cooked smoked sausage into bite-size rounds about ½ inch thick. Add to sauce, stirring to coat well. **Microwave method:** Cover lightly with waxed paper (you want the steam to vent) and cook 8 minutes on high, stirring halfway through. **Skillet method:** Bring the sauce and sausages to a bubbling simmer over medium heat. Cook uncovered for 15 minutes, stirring occasionally. Serve warm, accompanied by picks for spearing. Serves about 10.

STUFFED MUSHROOMS Buy and clean small, bite-size mushrooms, pluck out the stem, and stuff with any of the following: room temperature blue cheese, Brie, or Camembert (blended with a little softened butter and port until soft); OLIVADA (page 193); cooked crabmeat mixed with a little mayo or sour cream; pâté; chopped mushrooms and roasted nuts mixed with a little softened cream cheese; deli-bought caponata, ratatouille, baba ghanoush, taramasalata, or tabouli; whatever else is ready-made and soft enough to easily spoon into a mushroom.

TERRA CHIPS AND STIX A great alternative to potato and corn chips, Terra Chips are thin, crunchy slices (or sticks) of taro, sweet potatoes, yuca, batata, and parsnips. Terra also produces a variety of other chips, including blue potato, sweet potato, and Yukon gold. You can find them in most supermarkets.

Sharon Tyler Herbst, dubbed the foremost writer of user-friendly food and drink reference works, is an award-winning author of seventeen books. She gained her reputation as an accomplished culinary powerhouse with the bestseller *Food Lover's Companion,* broadly hailed as "A must for every cook's library." It, as well as *Wine Lover's Companion* (coauthored with her husband, Ron), are the on-line dictionaries on several major food-and-drink Internet sites. Julia Child praised Sharon's *Food Lover's Tiptionary* as "An invaluable help for all." TV's popular quiz show *Jeopardy* often cites Sharon's books as references. She is also a food and travel journalist and a media personality with myriad appearances on national radio and television shows, including *Good Morning America* and the *Today* show. She's a consultant and spokesperson for national food and beverage companies and a past president of the International Association of Culinary Professionals (IACP). Her Internet site is Food and Drink INK® (www.sharontylerherbst.com).